Book 2 ⋈ American Aircraft Series

Y0-BMG-772

CESSNA GUIDEBOOK

VOLUME I

by Mitch Mayborn and Bob Pickett

THE COVER. Rare Cessna photograph taken during 1944 or 1945 shows two company owned aircraft, C-165 (c/n 590, NC21938) and T-50 (c/n 1305A, NR32456). Completed July 18, 1941, (c/n 590) was the next to last C-165 built. It was repurchased by Cessna on May 27, 1942. It was recovered and repainted AN yellow with insignia blue trim and insignia red pinstripe on February 26, 1944, and it was destroyed Sept. 25, 1945 in a hangar fire at the Wichita Municipal airport. The T-50 is not as well documented and little is known of its operation.

FLYING ENTERPRISE PUBLICATIONS
3164 Whitehall • Dallas, Texas 75229

Library of Congress Catalog Number 72-89892
ISBN No. 0-912470-19-0

© Dallas, Texas, 1973 by
Flying Enterprise Publications.
All rights reserved.
2nd Edition, revised 1976

CESSNA GUIDEBOOK

VOLUME I

A CATALOG OF CESSNA AIRCRAFT, 1911 through 150L (1976 Model)

6 through 50

THE OLD ADVERTISING AND EDITORIAL SECTION

51 through 92

A history of the Cessna Aircraft Company. 2
How to use this book 4

APPENDIX

Cessna Geneology 93

PLANS & DRAWINGS

1911 Cessna 93
1917 Comet 93
Model AW 95
Model DC-6B 95
C-165 Airmaster (exploded) 98
C-165 Airmaster (3-view) 99
T-50 (cut-away) 100
T-50 (exploded) 100
T-50 (UC-78) 101
Model 120 102

Model 140A 102
Design Evolution of the 150 103
Cessna Racers 96-97

PERFORMANCE TABLES

1911 through GC-2 104
MW-1 through UC-78E 106
The 150 108

PRODUCTION DATA

Pre-War Aircraft construction numbers 110
Military serials 111

FLYING ENTERPRISE PUBLICATIONS

3164 Whitehall • Dallas, Texas 75229

American Aircraft Series

Book 1 — Stearman Guidebook
Book 2 — Cessna Guidebook (Vol. 1)
Book 3 — Ryan Guidebook
Book 4 — Grumman Guidebook (Vol. 1)

Library of Congress Catalog Number 72-89892
ISBN No. 0-912470-19-0

© Dallas, Texas, 1973 by
Flying Enterprise Publications.
All rights reserved.
2nd Edition, revised 1976

A HISTORY OF THE CESSNA AIRCRAFT COMPANY

FEBRUARY 11, 1911 was an important day for aviation, for it was then that an Enid, Oklahoma car dealer named Clyde V. Cessna saw an "Air Circus" at Oklahoma City. Cessna, a farmer, mechanic, salesman and dealer for Overland cars, became fascinated by the air show put on by the Moisant International Aviation Air Circus.

Bitten by the flying bug, and not unaware of the money paid to aviators for exhibition flying, Cessna went to New York and purchased a Bleriot built in the Bronx under license from the French Bleriot firm.

Assembling the airplane, and installing his own water-cooled engine, Cessna began to test fly the airplane and teach himself how to fly, for he had never flown an airplane before.

Setting up camp on the Great Salt Plains near Jet, Oklahoma, Clyde and his brother Roy spent weeks testing. Clyde survived a dozen crack-ups before achieving a straight flight on the thirteenth try. This flight too ended in a crash because Cessna had not yet learned how to turn the airplane. After several more attempts, and with several modifications to the airplane, Cessna made a completely successful flight and landing in June 1911.

Several months later, Cessna had mastered the art of flying the machine and booked an aerial exhibition at Jet, Oklahoma, being paid $300. He also gave three more exhibitions in the local area during 1911.

During the winter of 1911/1912, Cessna modified and rebuilt his airplane, and in the spring and summer months of 1912, he gave aerial demonstrations. Each winter from 1912 through 1915 Cessna would rebuild and improve his airplane; each summer and fall he gave flying demonstrations in the Kansas and Oklahoma areas.

In the fall of 1916, Cessna was lured to Wichita, Kansas by a local automobile manufacturer. He was offered space in the Jones Motor Car plant in return for painting the name of the Jones-Six car on the bottom of the wing of his new airplane. This airplane, built in the winter of 1916/1917 was the first airplane built in Wichita - known today as the Air Capital of the World because of the number of aircraft manufacturers headquartered there.

The next airplane built in Wichita was the 1917 Cessna Comet. This was his most successful airplane up to that time, and it featured a partially enclosed cockpit. Cessna had booked 30 exhibitions by July 1917, and expected to do 60 before the end of the year. However, America's entry into World War I curtailed his flying and he returned to his homestead near Rago, Kansas and to farming until 1925.

In that year, the flying bug struck Clyde Cessna again, and he returned to Wichita where he joined Walter Beech and Lloyd Stearman in founding the Travel Air Manufacturing Company; Cessna becoming president. A "design philosophy" conflict emerged; Cessna favored monoplanes — Beech favored biplanes. Only biplanes were being built at Travel Air, so in 1926, Cessna rented a small shop and designed and built a monoplane while still president of Travel Air. When he demonstrated the monoplane, Walter Beech was impressed and the 1926 Cessna monoplane thus became the basis of a series of very successful Travel Air monoplanes. The most famous of these were the "City of Oakland" and the "Woolaroc" which in 1927 were the first civilian airplanes to fly to Hawaii.

However, in early 1927 Cessna had resigned from Travel Air in order to establish his own designs featuring a full cantilever (strutless) monoplane, then a radical departure from accepted design practices. The new airplane was built in a small shop on West Douglas Street in Wichita. The airplane, the prototype to the "A" series of airplanes was an extremely clean design for the time.

Pleased with the performance of the new ship, Cessna organized a company and sold stock. A major stockholder, Victor Roos, joined with Cessna and the firm was organized as the Cessna-Roos Company on September 8, 1927. Eleven acres of land was purchased on First Street at Glenn Avenue, and a new 100 by 50 foot factory building - with a separate paint shop for safety reasons - was constructed for $35,000 in December. That same month, Victor Roos left the company to become general manager for Swallow, and the Cessna Aircraft Company, as it is still known in 1974, was incorporated on December 31, 1927.

Production got underway with the "A" series offered in five versions depending upon the engine selected. Work on the second basic Cessna model, the BW was also progressing. The BW was basically a beefed up AW with higher gross weight, However, the department of Commerce would not certify the BW as a 4-place airplane without a complete new stress analysis. So, the BW was sold as a 3-place airplane and design was speeded on the CW-6, a larger 6-place airplane with a 225 hp Wright J-5 engine.

In 1929, business looked good, and the company designed a fourth basic airplane, the DC-6. The 4-place model powered by a 300 hp engine was the DC-6A "Chief," the 225 hp version, the DC-6B "Scout". The DC-6 was the first airplane to be built at a new 80 acre plant on East Pawnee Road, just southeast of the Wichita city limits. Most of the single engine Cessnas are today being built at the same location, now the site of the Cessna Pawnee Division plant.

The Depression hit just as production was getting underway at the new 55,000 square foot facility, and sales dropped to almost nothing. To bolster sales, Cessna designed and built the CG-2 glider for $398.00, and there were a number of other small experimental Cessna airplanes built in an attempt to develop a marketable product suitable to depression pocketbooks.

However, in 1931, the plant was closed and the buildings rented. Although Cessna Aircraft did not go bankrupt,

The Jones Motor Car. Co. "Cessna" factory in 1917. Aircraft include, 1917 Comet (left), 1917 Cessna (middle) and 1915 Cessna (right).

2

it did not build any airplanes during 1931, 1932 or 1933.

During these years, Clyde Cessna and his son Eldon, prevented by the Board of Directors from building airplanes in the closed plant, opened a small shop on what later became the Stearman/Boeing-Wichita plant property. Here, operating as the C. V. Cessna Aircraft Company, they built three racers, the CR-1, CR-2 and CR-3, and a custom cabin job, the C-3.

In June 1933, Dwane L. Wallace, a nephew of Clyde Cessna, graduated from Wichita University with a degree in aeronautical engineering, and went to work for the Beech Aircraft Company, at that time renting a portion of the still closed Cessna plant. When Beech moved to its present location, Dwane Wallace and his brother Dwight persuaded the major stockholders of Cessna to reopen the plant. On January 10, 1934, Clyde Cessna was elected president, Dwight Wallace, treasurer and Dwane Wallace plant manager.

Armed with Dwane's aeronautical engineering knowledge and the practical design and manufacturing experience of Clyde and Eldon Cessna, they designed a new and highly efficient airplane, the C-34. A clean, modern airplane with cantilevered wings like its predecessors, the C-34 began to get the company on its feet. Demonstrating the airplane at air meets and races, test pilot George Hart and Dwane Wallace won races and garnered publicity for the company. Production of the C-34 picked up. Success was assured when a C-34 flown by Dwane Wallace won permanent possession of the Detroit News Trophy and the title "World's Most Efficient Airplane."

In 1935, Clyde sold his stock in the company to Dwane and Dwight Wallace, but remained as president until October 8, 1936 when he retired. Cessna returned to his homestead near Rago and farmed his 640 acres and invented farm implements until his death at 74, in 1954.

In 1938, design was started on Cessna's first twin-engined airplane, the T-50. Completed in nine months, the T-50 was test flown on March 26, 1939 by Dwane Wallace. Production of the T-50 had barely started when military orders for aircrew trainers took high priority, and the commercial T-50's yielded to silver AT-8's for the U.S. Army Air Corps and yellow Crane I's for the Royal Canadian Air Force.

Faced with the largest production orders ever received by Cessna, plant expansion grew by leaps and bounds. Employment grew from 200 in July 1940 to 1500 just seven months later. As the United States grew closer to war, even larger contracts were received for AT-17 trainers and later the UC-78 utility/cargo versions of that basic, pre-war T-50, a design that was the "right airplane at the right time" for Cessna.

While volume production of the Bobcat, as the T-50

Hand craftsmen at work on "Airmaster" wings in the mid-1930's.

Volume production at last. AT-17's await delivery in 1942.

series of airplanes was known, was in progress, single examples of several experimental airplanes were built, notably the T-50A, P-7 and P-10 twin-engine trainers.

In April 1942, Cessna received a contract to built 1500 Waco designed CG-4A troop/cargo gliders for the invasion of Europe. Cessna was designated prime contractor, responsible for procurement and coordination of production. A plant was hurriedly built at Hutchinson, Kansas, 60 miles northwest of Wichita. Other manufacturers in Wichita became subcontractors to Cessna. The bulk of the 750 gliders completed (750 were cancelled) were assembled and crated at the Boeing/Wichita plant while tooling was being built for the production of the secret B-29. Glider deliveries started in September, 1942, with 37; in October 234; in November 397; and December 81. The final 750th glider was delivered in January 1943. These Waco CG-4A gliders are not covered in this book since they were not actually "Cessna" aircraft.

Cessna designed a twin-engine cargo aircraft, the C-106. Made primarily of non-strategic war materials, a contract for 500 was received for the C-106A version. Before any aircraft were delivered, this order was cancelled due to the success of the Douglas C-47 and Curtis C-46 cargo planes. When Bobcat production was complete, Cessna built components for the vital Boeing B-29 and Douglas A-26 for the remainder of the war. Peak employment was 6074 people and production facilites grew from 55,000 square feet in 1939 to 468,000 square feet in 1944. Cessna won the Army-Navy "E" (for effort) Award five times, and did it without using any government loans or assistance.

As World War II drew near a conclusion, design was initiated on a "Family Car of the Air" for the forecasted air-minded America. The war in the Pacific was rapidly ending and the new design was shelved in favor of a new, but not so radical airplane that could be put into production more quickly. The result was the P-780, a fabric covered fuselage prototype of the Model 190/195 series. This aircraft, together with all other Cessna single engine airplanes, will be covered in the second volume of the Cessna Guidebook.

Cessna management noted that the first requirement of the returning serviceman would be inexpensive flight training, and thus the P-780 project was itself shelved in favor of the new model 120/140 two-seat lightplanes.

All metal (except for fabric covering on the wings) the 140, and the economy 120 were just what the market needed, and over the next several years a total of 7601 were built in several versions.

The two place market eventually became saturated by the large number of 120/140's sold, and the score of other light plane manufacturers trying to take advantage of the expected post-war aviation boom. When the boom did not develop as expected, sales fell off. Production of the

120/140 (on the same assembly line) fell from 30 airplanes a day to five per day.

As the two-place market filled up, Cessna management had the 190/195 ready, together with an all new four-place personal airplane, the Model 170.

A return to the two-place trainer market was made in 1959 with the new Model 150. Featuring all metal construction, tricycle landing gear, 100 hp, and pleasant flying characteristics, the 150 was an immediate success with flying schools, clubs and private pilots.

Production of the popular 150 reached 3000 per year in the 1966 model year and assembly of the 150 was shifted to Strother Field, near Winfield Kansas in late 1967. In 1969, during the business recession, the 150 production returned to Wichita until 1973, when the Strother Field plant was once more reactivated.

In 1966, production was started at Cessna's French affilate, Reims, Aviation. Sixty-seven were assembled that year. Since then, a total of 1224 F150 and Aerobat's have been produced at the Reims, France, facility. Altogether 18,435 Model 150's of all versions had been built by the end of the 1973 model year and the end is not in sight.

Arrangement of the book

The models are presented in approximate chronological sequence through 1945, with aircraft built in a particular time period being listed alphabetically for convenience. From that date, the airplanes are listed in Cessna model number sequence, 120, 140 and 150.

A History of Cessna Aircraft Model Numbers

The first two airplanes built by the Cessna-Roos Aircraft Company were recorded in official Department of Commerce records, as "Cessna-Roos Number 1 and Number 2," and alternately as "Cessna Design No. 1 and No. 2." After these two airplanes had been modified and re-engined, Cessna airplanes were identified by a code showing the number of seats and engine horsepower, i.e. "Cessna 4-120" was a four seater powered by a 120 hp Anzani engine.

Today the early production Cessna airplanes are popularly known by a two letter code. However, it was not until the early 1930's that this two letter code was officially used. Until that time Department of Commerce records show the Cessna airplanes simply as, "Cessna Cabin Monoplane." The two letter code evolved to provide better differentiation in models and these designations were retroactively applied to already produced airplanes. The first letter indicated the basic model. The second letter indicated the engine installed, A - Anzani, S - Siemens-Halske, etc.

This system broke down when optional engines were offered, such as the DC-6 (Fourth, or D series, Curtiss Challenger engine), DC-6A (300 hp Wright engine) and the DC-6B (255 hp Wright engine).

This "Basic Model" system lasted through the "G" series (GC-2 racer).

The airplanes and gliders build by Clyde and Eldon Cessna during the depression were designated "CR", etc, for Cessna Racer, "CG" for Cessna Glider and "CS" for Cessna Sailplane.

After the depression, the C-34 designation stood for Cessna - 1934, the the year design and construction began on the airplane. Thus, the C-37 was built in 1937, the C-38 in 1938. In 1938 the designation was changed to reflect the horsepower offered in the Airmaster, ie, C-145 and C-165 for the 145 hp or 165 hp engine.

It is thought that T-50 stood for Twin-engine-5 (place). The military model designations AT-8, AT-17, UC-78, JRC-1 and C-106 followed regular US Army Air Forces/US Navy designation systems. The experimental Cessnas were known by their Engineering Project number, such as P-7 and P-10. The C-106 was first known as the P260, or Project number 260, and it is unique in having an official AAF designation without ever having been accepted by the military.

The Post-War model designations were chosen more from a marketing standpoint than an engineering viewpoint. Model numbers were chosen that were easy to remember and that fit into an appropriate spot in a system that shows the entire Cessna family of airplanes. In this manner, the relationship of one model to another may be easily shown. Basically, the '100' series are the Light Single Engine airplanes; the '200' series, the Higher Powered Single engine airplanes; the '300' series, light twin-engine planes; the '400' series, larger twins; and the '500' series commercial jet airplanes.

Specialized airplanes such as the Agricultural airplanes and military models are also listed in their approximate place in this system.

Generally, a letter suffix indicates a significant yearly model change, such as Model 150A (1961), Model 150B (1962). The letters "O" and "I" are not normally used. A major engine change, or a change in the use of the airplane will normally result in a letter prefix to the model number, such as model A150K, for the model 150 Aerobat.

Serial Numbers

Cessna manufacturers serial numbers (referred to as Construction Number, or c/n) have followed several methods during the 45 years since the first production airplanes were built in 1927. It is not known if pre-World War 1 Cessnas had c/n's, but it is unlikely that they did.

The first airplanes built by Cessna-Roos in 1927 were apparently not serialized until the Department of Commerce (Forerunner of the CAA and FAA) began licensing airplanes and requiring the use of manufacturers serial numbers. When the first two Cessnas were licensed as X1626 and X1627, Cessna decided to use those numbers as the Cessna serial number (c/n). The Cessna airplanes of 1927 were issued c/n 1626-1633 which initially corresponded to the "Registration." It was soon obvious that

CESSNA AIRCRAFT COMPANY ORIGINAL MANUFACTURER'S SERIALS

C/N	Registration	Model	Engine	Remarks
1626	X1626	Design No. 1	Anzani (90 HP)	Built 10 Aug 1927 Registered as "Cessna-Roos No. 1". Rebuilt with 120 HP Anazi and assigned Cessna C/N 1628 (D.O.C. No. 4165)
1627	X1627	Design No. 2	Wright (200 HP)	Built 10 Sep 1927. Registered as "Cessna-Roos No. 1". Rebuilt with 125 HP Siemens and assigned Cessna C/N 1630 (D.O.C. No. 4157)
1628	4165	Cessna 4-120 (AA)	Anzani (120 HP)	Rebuilt C/N 1626. C/N later changed to C/N 112.
1629	4158	Cessna 4-200 (BW)	Wright J-4 (200 HP)	C/N changed to 113.
1630	4157	Cessna 4-125 (AS)	Siemens (125 HP)	Rebuilt C/N 1627 later changed to C/N 115.
1631	4156	Cessna (AA)	Anzani (120 HP)	C/N changed to 114.
1632				Possibly C/N changed to 116, 117, 118 or 119.
1633	4725	Cessna 4-200 (BW)	Wright J-5 (220 HP)	C/N changed to 120
116	5834	BW	Wright J-5 (220 HP)	
117	X5835	BW	Wright J-5 (220 HP)	
118	4724	BW	Wright J-5 (220 HP)	
119	5036	AA	Anzani (120 HP)	
120	4725	BW	Wright J-5 (220 HP)	Was C/N 1633

First Airplanes not designated Model AA, AW, AS, BW, etc, but were designated by No. of seats and engine horsepower.
Data based on letter, 18 July 1929, from Jesse W. Lankford, Chief, Licensing Section, D.O.C.

this system would not work as the D.O.C. numbers were not issued in blocks to a manufacturer. Due to much confusion in the records as which was the c/n and which was the registration, these airplanes were re-serialized, starting with c/n 112. Why start at c/n112? This is not known for certain. It is presumed that Clyde Cessna retroactively applied c/n100 through 112 to a combination of airplanes designed and built by him from 1911 to 1927. This is at best, conjecture, but it is the only plausible explanation that the authors could determine.

From c/n 112, the serials were consecutive, all models being included in the serial block c/n thru c/n 591, the end of Airmaster procuction. Not all c/n in this block were used, as production of a new model often began at a nice, round number (ie, C-38, c/n 400). c/n 592 thru c/n 599 were not used; c/n 600 to c/n 999 are reserved for experimental model; this block of numbers is still used today for that purpose.

T-50 series production began with c/n 1000, and went thru c/n 6700, the last UC-78 built. Again, not all the c/n's in this block were used nor were the airplanes always produced in c/n sequence.

For Post-War production, c/n blocks were allocated to the various models(c/n 7000/7999 for model 190/195, c/n 8000/8999 for Model 120/140. Because of the large quantities built, these c/n blocks were not sufficient, so additional c/n blocks were issue (ie, c/n 16,000/ 17,000 for the later Model 190/195). As production increased, still more c/n were needed. In 1961, the basic model number was added to the present c/n (172 c/n 47747 becoming c/n 17247747, for example) and this system is used today. All new models start with 0001 as in Model 185-0000 for the Model 185. In 1970, the "dash" was eliminated for computer purposes and an additional zero installed.

Twin-engine aircraft manufactured at the Wallace Division use a variation of the preceeding method: Each model year production is shown in a single block of c/n's, each new model starting with 0001 (ie, 1962 c/n 310G0001 thru 310G0156; 1963 c/n 310H0001 thru 310H0148, etc.)

Several military aircraft such as the T-41 (Model 172F) began life as versions of commercial models. These at first had c/n included in the basic model c/n block, but later production models had separate c/n blocks.

Cessna airplanes built at the Cessna Reims France affiliate, have separate serial blocks, with the letter F prefix (as in F1500001)

Aircraft are occasionally built out of c/n and military serial/registration number sequence. Thus, it is not always possible to interpolate to get a c/n from a given serial number, when the first and last c/n are known.

Model Year

Cessna airplanes are usually identified by a model year, rather than a calender year. Like automobiles, production of the next year's model begins prior to the beginning of the calendar year, so that deliveries may be made to dealers and distributors by the start of the model year. Thus, the early production models of the 1974 Model 150L were built in mid-year 1973. In this book then, "year of production" will refer to the model year, not the actual calendar year in which built.

While complete access to Cessna company records was granted to the authors, it should be pointed out that all data is the result of years of research by the authors, who take sole responsibility for the accuracy of this book. Cessna and FAA records were studied at length, yet some differences, particularly on the pre-war airplanes could not be resolved. In these cases, the authors used that data which could be best supported. Readers are invited to submit data and photos which may fill in missing data.

ACKNOWLEDGEMENTS AND PHOTO CREDITS

The authors would like to thank the Cessna Aircraft Company for its cooperation, and the use of its historical files. All photos, unless otherwise credited, are Cessna photos from the Authors' collections.

We also express our appreciation to Gerald Deneau whose research into the early Cessnas provided the foundation upon which this book is built. The excellent Cessna racer drawings were provided by noted air racing artist and historian, Robert S. Hirsch.

A number of individuals and organizations assisted in the preparation of this book. We would like to thank . . . **H. G. Anderson** for examples of early advertising; **Gary C. Arlington; Peter M. Bowers; Erwin J. Bulban; Leroy Burgess,** Cessna Engineering; **Merna Cherrett** of Cessna Quality Control Records; **Richard Currie; John M. Davis** of Air Britain; **E. M. Johnson,** Jr, for examples of early advertising; GM Research Labs, courtesy Special-Interest Autos Magazine, Box 196, Bennington, Vermont 05201 for the C-165 GM Special photograph, (page 30); **Don Hannah; Jerry Kell,** Cessna Public Relations Director; **Michael Lamm; William T. Larkins** for the JRC-1 photo (page 36); **Tom Shockey,** administrative engineer, Cessna Pawnee Division; **Rod Simpson** of Air Britain; **Ray Stegman,** Cessna Pawnee Division photo lab for many of the prints, but especially for his work in processing the CS-1 photos (page 17) from old movie film; **John Underwood** for photographs of the AF (page 12), the GC-2 (page 20) and the CR-1 (page 21); and **Larry Wiggins,** photo editor for Cessna.

The Authors

Bob Pickett   **Mitch Mayborn**

Bob Pickett was born in Wichita, Kansas in 1937. Presently he is Operational Auditor for the Cessna Corporate Office, and is the official Cessna historian. Bob has spent many years and hundreds of hours compiling Cessna data, and this is the first major publication of his work. He served with the USAF Auditor General Office from 1961-1965 following graduation from Wichita University in 1960. Bob is a founder of the Wichita Scale Aircraft Modelers Association. He was National Treasurer for IPMS-USA (1970-72), and is a member of Air Britain, and American Aviation Historical Society.

Mitch Mayborn *was born in Temple, Texas in 1936. Presently he is Editor and Publisher of Flying Enterprise Publications, and editorial consultant for Associated Publishers, Inc. Mitch is a pilot, with a commercial license and multi-engine and instrument ratings and is an A&P mechanic. He flew the Grumman G-159 and Convair 240, two years for Dresser Industries, Inc. Presently he owns a 1940 Ryan STM-S2 (STA Special). Mitch spent 10 years as Managing Editor of Drilling Magazine. He has contributed many historical aviation articles to national aviation magazines and has published several books. Mitch lives in Dallas with his wife Corinne and children, Ellen, Susan and Neal. He is a member of the EAA, Antique Airplane Association, CAHA, AAHS, AWA and the Texas Aviation Historical Society.*

1911 Cessna   **1 built, 1911**

Inspiration for Clyde Cessna's venture into aviation came from his visit to the Moisant International Aviators Air Circus at Oklahoma City, February 11, 1911. Cessna, already a skilled automotive mechanic, journeyed to New York, and purchased a Bleriot monoplane (less engine) from the Queens Airplane Company (New York), U. S. licensee for the French Bleriot company. Returning to Kansas, Clyde installed a 60 hp, 4 cylinder watercooled Elbridge engine which always overheated. Cessna started his "do it yourself" flying lessons near Jet, Oklahoma that spring. Often crashing, it was not until the 13th attempt that he succeeded. After each crash, the airplane had been rebuilt and modified, so that by the time Cessna first flew, the machine was for all practical purposes a "Cessna." Photo at Cherokee, Oklahoma Fair Ground, Oct 1911.

1912 Cessna "Silver Wings"   **1 built, 1912**

During the winter months of 1911-12, Clyde Cessna rebuilt and improved his original 1911 airplane. Reliability was improved with the installation of a 40 hp aircooled Anzani radial, and the landing gear was modified to include a buggy spring shock absorber. Clyde Cessna and his 1912 "Silver Wings" was the star attraction at county fairs and local gatherings throughout Northern Oklahoma and Southern Kansas. Photograph was taken near Enid, Oklahoma, April 14, 1912.

1913 Cessna   **1 built, 1913**

Cessna's 1913 airplane was a further refinement of the earlier machines which he had built. Again powered with a 40 hp aircooled Anzani radial, the main changes to the 1913 airplane included a redesigned and simplified landing gear and a revised wing support parallel to the air flow. The fuselage was covered by fabric for the first time. Dimensions of the aircraft remained the same. Clyde Cessna continued his performance at airshows and exhibitions in Kansas and Oklahoma during the summer of 1913.

1914 Cessna (1915)   **1 built, 1914; modified 1915**

Improvements in 1914 included further refinements in the rigging and superstructure and the landing gear. But the most obvious improvement was a simple windshield which made its first appearance on a Cessna. The photo above, taken at Burdett, Kansas shows the small windshield just below the triangular supports. Engine was the same 40 hp Anzani. In 1915 the old Elbridge engine made it's re-appearance on this airframe.

1917 Cessna (Jones Six)　　　1 built, fall 1916

The first airplane built in Wichita, Kansas was Clyde Cessna's first 1917 airplane. Built at the Jones Motor Car plant, Clyde was offered factory space and the use of woodworking tools in trade for painting a large JONES SIX on the underside of the left wing. The Jones Six was a car built in Wichita by Mr. J. J. Jones., who had been an acquaintance of Clyde Cessna's from his automotive days. The landing gear, wing braces and control wires were further refined. Wingspan was 27 ft, length 21 ft 6-in. and the height was 8 ft, the first dimensional change in the airplanes. Engine was the old standby, 6 cylinder Anzani aircooled radial.

1917 Cessna (Comet)　　　1 built, 1917

Final refinement of the early Cessna series is the Comet, second aircraft built in Wichita, and last of the airplanes built by Clyde Cessna for nine years. The Comet had the 40 hp Anzani engine. Most obvious feature was the partially enclosed cockpit for the first time. This was the last Cessna to use wing warping for control. In the Comet, Clyde Cessna set a United States speed record of 124.62 mph on July 5, 1917 in a flight from Blackwell, Oklahoma to Wichita, covering the 75 miles in 36½ minutes. Clyde stands by his Comet in typical flying attire of the 1917 period.

1926 Cessna monoplane Experimental 1 built, 1926

The first high wing, conventional cabin monoplane designed by Clyde Cessna was built as a result of a disagreement on the advantages of the monoplane with Walter Beech while both men were at Travel Air. At the time, Cessna was president of the company. However he designed and, with a couple of helpers, built the 1926 airplane in a shop on West Douglas Avenue in Wichita during 1926 and early 1927. This aircraft was essentially the prototype for the Travel Air 5000. Engine was a 120 hp Anzani aircooled radial and there were accomodations for four people. Final disposition unknown.

Cessna Design No. 1 Experimental/Racing 1 built, 1927

Completed Aug 10, 1927, the first airplane built by the Cessna-Roos Aircraft Company was called simply "Cessna Design No. 1." It was built at the same time as "Design No. 2" described on the next page. Shown smiling from the cockpit of the 90 hp Anzani powered Design No. 1 (c/n 1626) is Clyde Cessna. The photograph was taken Aug 20, 1927 and the Department of Commerce (D.O.C.) identification number X1626 has not been applied. Early records are confused, however it is thought that this aircraft (Design No. 1, c/n 1626, D.O.C. No. X1626) was subsequently modified with the installation of an Anzani 120 hp engine and assigned a different c/n 1628 with D.O.C. No. 4165. As Cessna and the D.O.C. got their records straight, it was later changed to c/n 112 and known as the model AA.

Cessna Design No. 2　　　　　　　　**Experimental/Racing**　　　　　　　　**1 built, 1927**

Previously believed to be modification of the first Cessna-Roos airplane illustrated on page 9, research for this book shows conclusively that this airplane, D.O.C. Identification No. 1627 was a completely different airplane built concurrently with No. 1626 and completed a month later on September 10, 1927. Mounting a 200 hp Wright Whirlwind engine, the Cessna Design No. 2 was initially licensed X1627. "Design No. 2" was a 3-seater with a single circular window on each side of the cabin, and it had a door on both sides while Design No. 1 had a door only on the left. Other changes included an enclosed cockpit, the fuselage was less rounded and the wing was mounted on top of the fuselage, rather than shoulder mounted. In the photograph above, taken Oct. 6 1927, Design No. 2 (c/n 1627, D.O.C. 1627) is shown as originally built. This same aircraft later became Design No. 2 (modified) with a new serial (c/n 1630) and still later it became model AS (new c/n 115).

Cessna Design No. 2 (modified)　　　　　　**Experimental**　　　　　　**1 modified, 1927**

By December 1, 1927, the Design No. 2 (c/n 1627, D.O.C. 1627) as shown above, was modified by adding cabin windows and installing a 10 cylinder Anzani. Note the different style of lettering on the fuselage and the position of the Cessna "bird" emblem on the tail. Essentially a production prototype for the "A" series, this cabin version of Design No. 2 was licensed as a three place airplane with a gross weight of 2260 lbs, and a top speed of 130 mph. During December 1927 and January 1928 work was undertaken to modify and re-engine Design No. 2 with a 125 hp Siemens-Halske engine. This conversion of c/n 1627 resulted in the first model "AS" with a new c/n assigned 1630 and D.O.C. identification 4157 (see "AS").

AA   ATC 65 (Aug 27, 1928)   15 (14 built, 1 modified) 1928

Shown above is AA (c/n 114, 4156) which was sold to E. A. Link (later to develop the Link trainer) on February 28, 1928. Photo taken February 22. List price of the AA was $6300 with a wooden prop or $6500 with a metal one. First AA airplanes were produced and sold with the ATC certificate pending. After issuance, some modifications had to be made to the gear of the first produced aircraft. Note unusual position of the Cessna "bird" under the front cabin window. Span of the AA was 40 ft 2-in. and length was 25 ft 6-in. Top speed was 130 mph with a 120 hp Anzani engine.

AC   ATC 65 (Aug 27, 1928)   1 built, 1928

Engine installation determined the suffix to the "A" type. The "AC" was thus a 130 hp Comet air cooled radial engine. One aircraft was built as an "AC", (c/n 150, NC6450) and the original selling price was $7000. The "A" series of Cessna airplanes marked the first major production by the new company. The "A" series of aircraft were built of welded steel tubing fuselage and the wings were an all wood structure. Over all was fabric covering. This was the "standard" Cessna method of construction until the post war 190/195 series. The "A" seated four and the maximum gross weight was 2260 pounds.

AF Special Memo 2-237 (July 17, 1930) 3 built, 1928

Three "AF" types (c/n 137,141,149) were produced in 1928 with the 150 hp Axelson (Floco) engine. Essentially the same as other "A" series aircraft, the "AF" ("F" for Floco) originally sold for $7200. Second "AF" sold went to the Axelson Machine Company of Los Angeles, California, manufacturer of the Floco engine. This aircraft (c/n 141) is shown above bearing identification number 7462 in a rare photograph showing an "AF" for the first time. Length of the "AF" was 24 ft 10½-in. Gross weight was the same as other "A" types at 2260 pounds and the empty weight was 1554 pounds, for the three place airplane.

AS Memo 2-8 (Jan 5, 1928) 4 (3 built, 1 modified) 1928

Cessna design No. 2 was further modified and a 125 hp Siemens-Halske engine installed. The airplane was called a Cessna 4-125 (4 place, 125 hp) by February 9, 1928 when the above photo was taken. Originally Cessna c/n 1627, D.O.C. 1627, this was changed to c/n 1630 D.O.C. 4157 when it was modified to the AS configuration. Later a new system was adopted by Cessna resulting in c/n 1630 being cancelled and a new c/n 115 assigned. D.O.C. number remained 4157. It was not until several years later that it was officially called a Model AS. Official D.O.C. records show references to "Cessna Cabin Monoplane" and advertising bears this out. Four A's were built, (c/n 115 (modified from Design No. 2) and c/n 123, 136 and 139). C/n 115, illustrated above was sold April 28, 1928 to Beacon Airways of Kansas City, Missouri, Original price was $7200 or $7525 with a metal prop. Registration 4157 (c/n 115) expired in 1936 and the airplane disappeared from sight.

AW   ATC 72 (Sept 7, 1928)   48 built, 1928-July 1929

Most popular of the "A" series was the 110 hp Warner powered "AW"; 47 were built during 1928 through July 1929, with one additional being completed May 1930. The "AW" was one of the least expensive "A" types at $6900. It had a 110 mph cruise speed with 110 hp. The first AW (c/n 140, NC 7107) flew in the National Air races where it appeared with Number 99. Flying c/n 140, Earl Rowland won the New York Los Angles Air Derby in 1928. In May 1929, the same airplane with Parker Cramer piloting, flew New York to Nome, Alaska to East Cape, Siberia and back to New York. Length of the "AW" was 24 ft 8½-in., empty weight 1225 pounds. Shown is c/n 151, NC 9091, photo taken January 28, 1929.

BW   Memo 2-7 (Dec 16, 1928)   12 built, 1928

The "BW" was basically a beefed-up "A" with a 220 hp Wright J-5 engine; the first was delivered March 28, 1928. The Department of Commerce would not approve the "BW" as a four place airplane because of a higher gross weight than the original ATC allowed, unless a complete recertification program was undertaken. Cessna chose to remove one of the front seats, sell the "BW" as a 3-place, and terminate production after building 12 airplanes. It was easier to build a completely new design instead of recertifying an old one. Photograph shows "BW" c/n 138, NC6442, taken November 6, 1928.

CW-6   **Experimental**   **1 built, 1928**

Cessna's first six-passenger airplane was the 3950 pound gross weight CW-6 (c/n 146, 6446) which was completed November 1, 1928. Powered by a 220 hp Wright J-5, the CW-6 ("C" for the third Cessna model, "W" for Wright and "6" for six passenger) is shown on exhibit February 16, 1929 at the 1929 Auto Show at the Wichita Forum. Original price was $14,500. While on a demonstration tour of Mexico, the CW-6 was confiscated by the government and reportedly used to drop bombs on rebels. Cessna pilot Earl Rowland was detained a week then given a receipt for the airplane and released. The Mexican government later paid for the aircraft but its final fate is unknown.

DC-6   **ATC 207 (Aug 19, 1929)**   **5 built, 1929**

Photograph shows the first DC-6 (c/n 157, 8142) on April 3, It was one of the last planes built at the original Cessna plant before Cessna moved into the new plant on East Pawnee Road. The four-place DC-6 originally listed for $9200 and there were five built during 1929. Original engine was the 170 hp R-600 Curtiss Challenger engine, however all but the first airplane shown above, were subsequently re-engined with the 225 hp Wright J-6 becoming the same as the DC-6B.

DC-6A "Chief"   ATC 243 (Sept 30, 1929)   22 built, 1929-1930

After testing the DC-6 it was decided to improve performance by changing to the 300 hp Wright R-975 Whirlwind engine. This increase of 130 hp gave the DC-6A a cruise speed of 130 mph (top 161) compared to a cruise of 105 (top 130) for the DC-6. Twenty-two DC-6A aircraft are accounted for; however records from this period are incomplete and additional aircraft were possibly built. Four DC-6A were impressed during WWII as the UC-77 (AAF s/n 42-38290, 42-46637/39). Photo shows DC-6A (c/n 199, 9864) on June 7, 1929. List price was $11,500. An 18 year-old pilot, Stanley Boynton, flew a DC-6A from Maine to California in just under 24 hours and returned in 20 hours nine minutes, setting a record for "junior pilots." A DC-6A placed 14th in the National Air Tour of 1929.

DC-6B "Scout"   ATC 244 (Sept 30, 1929)   22 built, 1929-1930

The DC-6B was slightly less powerful, being powered with the 225 hp (250 at take-off) Wright R-760 Whirlwind. There are 22 DC-6B accounted for in production records, and four additional DC-6 airplanes were converted to the DC-6B configuration. Four DC-6B were impressed during WWII as the UC-77A (AAF s/n 42-38292/95.) Photo shows DC-6B (c/n 211, C631K) on September 28, 1929. Cruise was 120 mph, top speed 146. Selling price of the 4-place, 3100 pound gross weight DC-6B was $10,000.

CG-2 No ATC 300 built, 1929-1930

In an attempt to keep the company from going bankrupt during the depression, Cessna designed and built the CG-2, a $398.00 training glider. After an initial CG-1 (Cessna Glider, c/n 1, 649K) reportedly 300 of the production CG-2 (c/n 2, N304M shown) were built. There are a confirmed 84 construction numbers accounted for. Possibly some were built and not ever licensed. The CG-2, with a 35 ft 2-in. wingspan and a length of 18 ft, served as the basis for the CPG-1, the EC-2 and the CS-1.

CPG-1 Experimental 1 built, 1930

The Cessna Powered Glider (CPG-1) was modified from CG-2 (c/n 39, N344M) in April 1930. It was powered by a 10 hp Cleone engine, shown mounted behind the pilot on the fuselage-something Cessna is still doing in 1973! CPG, with a 5 quart fuel capacity was the forerunner of the Baby Cessna. A lot of the work with the gliders was done by Eldon Cessna, Clyde's son.

CS-1   **Experimental**   **1 built, 1930**

The CS-1 (for Cessna Sailplane) was one more attempt to get a marketable product in the air during the height of the depression. Shown in flight is the only CS-1 (c/n 18, N322M) at the Cessna Pawnee plant in 1930. Very little is known about the CS-1, although its long "sailplane" wing is evident in this photograph. It was based on the CG-2 glider and featured a fully cantilever wing. Piloting the CS-1 is Eldon Cessna. The very rare photograph published above was taken from a recently discovered 1930 movie, which accounts for the rather scratchy quality. This is the first time that a photograph of the CS-1 has ever been published. Another view is in the "scrapbook" section of this book.

Baby Cessna   **Experimental**   **1 built, 1930**

Basically a "covered" CG-2, the Baby Cessna (c/n 77, 133V) was an attempt to develop a truly low priced "everyman's" airplane. Eldon Cessna converted a CG-2 by enclosing the fuselage, making a tiny cabin, adding a 25 hp Cleone engine, landing gear and cantilever wing. True to its glider heritage, the little craft had the same 35 ft 2-in. wingspan and approximately 18 ft length of the CG-2.

EC-1   **Experimental**   **3 built, 1930**

The EC-1 was a one-place, cleaned up and refined Baby Cessna, powered with a 25 hp Cleone engine. The photograph shows EC-1 (c/n 251, N403W) with competition number 115 on the side. There were three built, c/n 71, 199V; c/n 77, 133V; and c/n 251, N403W, later converted into the first EC-2. C/n 71 was re-engined in August 1930 with a home-built engine designed by John Self. Possibly a fourth EC-1 was built (c/n 250) but records do not confirm this.

EC-2   **Experimental**   **2 built, 1930-1931**

The ultimate in design evolution of the Cessna gliders was the pretty, 2-place EC-2 powered by the 30 hp Aeronca E-107A engine. The second EC-2 (c/n 253, N405W shown) was the last airplane built by Cessna Aircraft Company before the Board of Directors closed the plant to wait out the end of the depression. The first EC-2 (c/n 251) completed July 25, 1930 was modified from the EC-1.

FC-1   **Experimental**   **1 built, 1930**

Owned and flown by Eldon Cessna, the FC-1 was a progressive development of the Baby Cessna and was built about the same time as the EC-1, being essentially the same except for the change to a 95 hp inverted American Cirrus Ensign engine. The FC-1 (c/n 248, N138V) was completed on June 19, 1930 as a two place airplane.

CPW-6 (Goebel Special)   **Experimental (Racer)**   **1 built, 1929**

Designed as an endurance racing airplane for Art Goebel who won the Dole Air Derby (San Francisco/Honolulu, 1927) the CPW-6 (c/n 190, R9355) was basically a CW-6 redesigned to accomodate a Pratt & Whitney 420 hp Wasp engine supplied by Goebel. In addition to fairing the fuselage into a circular section, the CPW-6 had a 600 gallon fuel tank installed and a crew of two. Completed May 1, 1929 the "Goebel Special" was entered in a race from San Francisco to New York, but did not compete due to a fuel leak which developed the day before the race. The sole CPW-6 was converted to the CW-6 configuration and was destroyed in a hangar fire in late 1929. Gross weight was 4250 lb, wingspan 43 ft, length 30 ft 3-3/8-in. Top speed 160, cruise 130.

GC-1   **Experimental (Racer)**   **1 built, 1930**

The Cirrus All American Air Derby (1930) was a $25,000 prize, 5541 mile cross country race. Only airplanes with Cirrus engines were eligible so Cessna designed the GC-1 (c/n 249, NR144V) with a 110 hp American Cirrus Ensign, an inverted, supercharged 310 cu. in. engine. Wings and tail were indentical to the FC-1. Fuselage was small, accomodating a pilot no larger than 135 lb and 5 ft 7-in. The GC-1 sold for $3500 on July 9, 1930 to the Blackwell Oklahoma Aviation Corp. Pilot Stan Stanton, shown here, won one leg of the race, placing 7th overall. After the Cirrus Derby the supercharger was removed and the GC-1 was flown by Earl Smith placing 4th in the 1000 cu. in. event at the 1930 National Air Races with a speed of 137.4 mph. The GC-1 was destroyed in a hangar fire at Blackwell in March 1932.

GC-2   **Experimental (Racer)**   **1 built, 1930**

Identical to the GC-1 except for a 110 hp Warner radial, with full NACA cowl, the GC-2 (c/n 252, NR404W) was built for the 1930 National Air Races. The front of the fuselage was shortened and refaired to streamline with the radial Warner. The GC-2 was sold to Earl Rowland on August 14, 1930 for $2000 (less engine). Flown by Bill Ong and May Haizlip, the GC-2 placed second in the 450 and 650 cu. in. events, third in the 800 cu. in. race and second in the Woman's Free-For-All event. The GC-2 had a wingspan of 27 ft and a length of 20 ft 5-in. Final disposition is not known and there are no other race records recorded for the GC-2.

MW-1 **Experimental (Racer)** **1 built, 1929**

One of the least known Cessna airplanes is the MW-1 (c/n 195, X9860). It was built in July 1929, reportedly by Cessna employees from a wrecked AW, which it closely resembles except for the mid-wing and the closely cowled Wright J-5 of 225 hp. Also known as the CM-1, the airplane had a wingspan of 36 ft and a length of 20 ft 10-in. It is shown here bearing a racing number 95.

CR-1 **Experimental (racer)** **1 built, 1932**

Clyde and Eldon Cessna once again teamed up on a racer, and as the C. V. Cessna Aircraft Company, they produced their first retractable landing-gear airplane, the CR-1. Powered by the 125 hp Warner radial, the stubby (14 ft 6-in. long) CR-1 turned in a speed of 176.519 mph when flown by Roy Liggett at the National Air Races in Cleveland, 1932, placing third in the 510 cu in. event. Named "Miss Wanda" in honor of Clyde's daughter, the CR-1 (c/n 1, 11711) had a wingspan of 18 ft 6-in.

CR-2 (CR-2A) Experimental (racer) 1 modified, 1933

In 1933, Eldon redesigned the CR-1. It was renumbered CR-2 and assigned c/n 2. The fuselage was lengthened to 17 ft, engine changed to 145 hp Warner and empenage enlarged. Still named "Miss Wanda", the CR-2, piloted by Roy Liggett, won the Col. Green Cup Race at the 1933 Miami Air Races. At the Aero Digest Trophy Race (1933) the CR-2 flown by Art Davis, was second only to the newer CR-3, clocking 202.88 mph. Sold to R. O. Herman, the CR-2 was further modified, becoming CR-2A. Changes included a tight fitting engine cowl with streamlined bumps to clear rocker boxes. This cowling came loose at 300 ft during a high speed run at the 1933 International Air Races and tore off the left wing, killing pilot Roy Liggett and destroying the CR-2A.

CR-3 Experimental (racer) 1 built, 1933

In a short two-month period before it was destroyed, the CR-3 (c/n 3 NR57Y) won every race in which it was entered. It established a world speed record (engines less than 500 cu in.) clocking an average speed of 237.7 mph for four laps, beating the 213.8 mph record established by Benny Howard in "Ike." Had it lasted longer, the CR-3 might have become one of the most famous racers of all time. The CR-3 was designed especially for Johnny Livingston. It cost $2700 less the 145 hp Warner and prop supplied by him. It flew June 11, 1933 and was destroyed August 1 when Livingston abandoned it at Columbus, Ohio when the landing gear would not extend. Top speed was 255 mph. Gross weight 750 lb. Wingspan was 18 ft 6-in and length 17 ft.

C-3 Memo 2-473 1 built, 1933

The C-3 was the fourth and last airplane built by the C. V. Cessna Aircraft Company during the "hibernation" of the Cessna Aircraft company. The one C-3 (c/n 4, NC12568) was an extensive modification to AA (c/n 124, NC5335). Changes included installation of a NACA cowled 125 hp Warner engine, a wider 4-place cabin and use of a DC-6 type landing gear. The 2280 lb gross weight C-3 had an adjustable propeller. Originally built for Walt Anderson (White Castle Hamburger Stands) the C-3 was later bought by Marcellus Murdock, then publisher of the Wichita Eagle.

C-34 (Production) ATC 573 (summer 1935) 42 built, 1935-36 (includes prototype)

The second C-34 (c/n 255, NX14425) on wing to XB-AJO on fuselage, is shown here on November 22, 1935, bearing both registrations. Aircraft had been registered as NX14425 and when sold to Ross Colley of Tuxpan, Mexico it was re-registered XB-AJO. This aircraft was delivered to Mexico from Kansas at a cost of $15.24 in fuel averaging 16.9 mpg. Of the C-34's built, 9 were exported; two to England and to South Africa, and one each to Mexico, Argentina, Australia, Canada and Portugal. During WWII, 2 C-34's were impressed into the AAF as UC-77B (c/n 309 as s/n 42-78025 and c/n 321 as 42-78021). Additional C-34 descriptions on the following page.

C-34 (Prototype) ATC 573 (summer 1935) 1 built, 1935

The C-34 design was initiated in 1934 and the prototype C-34 (c/n 254, NC12599) is shown at the factory June 1, 1935. Certification followed shortly and there were 9 built in 1935 and 33 built in 1936. Powered by a 145 hp Warner Super Scarab 7 cylinder radial, the C-34 had a speed of 162 mph at sea level and 143 mph on 75 percent power at 8200 ft. The first Cessna to use wing flaps, the basic C-34 was to provide the basis for a whole generation of Cessna airplanes, its design traceable through the postwar 190/195 series. The first C-34 was still active in 1973. The $4995, 4-place C-34 had a service ceiling of 18,900 ft, a range of 535 miles with 35 gallons or 785 miles with an optional 52½ gallon installation.

C-34   ATC 573 (summer 1935)   42 built, 1935-36 (includes prototype)

Built June 1, 1936, C-34 (c/n 320, N15852) was given racing number 75 and used as a company demonstrator and race plane. Painted PPG "Pee Wee" green with "Chrome Yellow" trim and "Medium Yellow" pinstriping, the C-34 shown here September 10, 1936 looked as good as it flew. With George Hart as pilot, the C-34 entered and won the Detroit News Trophy Race of 1935. Ensuing publicity helped boost production to 3 airplanes per month in 1936. In 1936 with Dwane Wallace at the controls the C-34 again won the Detroit News Trophy Race at the All American Air Races in Miami. Winning both the 1935 and 1936 races earned the C-34 the title "World's Most Efficient Airplane", and permanent possession of the Detroit News Trophy. Eldon Cessna won in 1931 in an "AW"; there were no races in 1932-1934.

C-37   ATC 622   46 built, 1936-1937

Factory demonstrator, C-37 (c/n 356, NC17086) is shown on April 9, 1937. Subsequently this aircraft was sold to Reed Pigman of El Paso, Texas. This was the 6th C-37 and was painted PPG Cream, a Cedar stripe and Drake Blue pinstripe. Eight of the 46 C-37's were exported; 2 to Canada and the Philippines and 1 each to Australia, West Africa, Norway and Finland. The Finnish C-37 (c/n 385, OH-VKF) was later impressed into the Finish Air Force as s/n CE-1. Price of the 4-place C-37 was $5490. Dimensions were identical to the C-34 with wingspan 34 ft 2-in., length 24 ft 8-in. and gross weight 2350 lb. Service ceiling was 18,900 ft and range 525 miles with 35 gallon tank or 785 with an optional 52½ gallon tank. Additional C-37 descriptions on the following page.

C-37 (Prototype)　　　　　　　　　　　ATC 622　　　　　　　　　　　　1 built, 1936

The C-37 was a refined version of the C-34 with main differences being a 5-in. wider cabin at the top, new cowling, electric wing flaps and improved shock absorbers. The prototype (c/n 330, NC17070) is shown above on December 9, 1936 as it first appeared. Below it has been certified and the "X" changed to "NC". Color of first C-37 was Medium Yellow with Marine Blue letters and trim and gold pinstriping. Engine on the C-37 was the 145 hp Warner Super Scarab. Performance was similar to the C-34 with a top speed of 162 mph at sea level, 143 mph at 75 percent power at 8200 ft.

C-37 (camera plane)   ATC 622

A special camera version of the C-37 was built with windows forward of the cabin and an additional camera window in the belly. Shown here is C-37 (c/n 366, NC18047) on July 26, 1937. This camera plane was later impressed into the AAF as UC-77D (s/n 42-78024). Original paint was International Orange, Marine Blue trim with a Gold pinstripe. Production of the C-37 reached a high of 7 per month in June. C-37's were also equipped with floats and skis. Two additional C-37's were impressed into the AAF. These were c/n 347 AF s/n 42-97412 and c/n 381 AF s/n 42-78023. A total of 23 "Airmaster" versions were delivered as photo airplanes as follows: C-37 (7); C-38 (6); C-145 (2); and C-165 (8).

C-38 "Airmaster"   ATC 668   16 built, 1937-1938

The first C-38 (c/n 400, NC18048) shown here December 24, 1937, was completed on October 11. C-38 had the same 145 hp Warner Super Scarab engine as the earlier airplanes, but differed from the C-37 in that it had a hydraulically operated fuselage flap in place of the electrically operated wing flaps, curved landing gear legs offering a 12-in. wider tread, a larger vertical fin and plexiglass in place of the earlier pyrolin windshield. Production on the C-38 was terminated in August when the C-145 was introduced. The C-38 was the first airplane to officially be called "Airmaster" a term that is presently used for all Cessna airplanes from C-34 through C-165.

C-38 "Airmaster"   ATC 688

Shown here on March 18, 1938, just six days after completion is C-38 (c/n 403, NC18496) the fourth built. Painted Pee Wee Green with Royal Maroon trim and Ivory pinstriping, this Airmaster was later, along with C-38 (c/n 414) modified to C-145 configuration by the installation of the C-145 wing and removal of the belly flap. Six of the C-38 were equipped with camera provisions similar to the earlier described C-37. Top speed was 162 mph at sea level, cruise 151 mph at 75 percent power at 8200 ft and the C-38 had a service ceiling of 18,000 ft. Wingspan was 34 ft 2-in., length was 24 ft 8-in. Gross weight was 2350 lb and cost of the 4-place C-38 was $6490.

C-145 "Airmaster"   ATC 701   42 built, 1938-1941

The model designation system was changed with the C-145, indicating engine hp instead of model year. Difference between the C-145 and the C-38 was installation of electric split-flaps installed in the mid-chord position on the underside of the wings, and Cessna's first use of hydraulic brakes. Performance was the same as the C-38, with dimensions identical. 1941 prices for the C-145 were $7875 for the standard version, $8315 for the photo version and $10,635 for the floatplane. Photo above shows C-145 prototype (c/n 450, NC19464) on September 11, 1938, the day after its completion. Color was Brilliant Vermilion, Drake Blue trim and Marine Blue pinstripe.

C-145 "Airmaster" ATC 701

The third C-145 (c/n 452) is shown on October 5, 1938 the day after completion. Aircraft was named "Queimado II" and purchased by Ignacio Nogueira of Rio de Janiero, Brazil where it was registered as PP-TEH. Original paint was overall Aluminum, trim was Deep Vermilion and pinstripe was Marine Blue. There were a total of 3 C-145's exported, one each to Brazil, Finland (c/n 464) and Puerto Rico (c/n 576). The C-145 and C-165 airplanes were produced simultaneously and the c/n's are not consecutive for each model during this period.

C-165 "Airmaster" ATC 701 38 built, 1939-1942

Identical to the C-145 except for the more powerful 165 hp Warner Super Scarab, the C-165 had an increase in performance over the C-38 and C-145's. Top speed was 165 mph at sea level and the cruise speed was increased to 157 mph at 75 percent power at 8200 ft. Service ceiling was 19,300 ft, while range was 485 miles with a 35 gallon tank, and 725 with an optional 52½ gallon installation. Shown here is C-165 (c/n 583, NC32450) in early February 1941. Known as "Dwane's airplane", this C-165 is presently in storage at the Cessna Wallace Division plant. C-165's sold for $8275 for the landplane, $8715 photo version and $11,035 floatplane. There were 3 C-165's acquired by the AAF as UC-94 (c/n 558, 562, 591 as AAF s/n 42-78018, 42-78022 and 42-107400).

C-165 "General Motors Special" Experimental 1 built, 1940

Cesna adapted the basic C-165 airframe to take the installation of an experimental General Motors X-250 liquid cooled engine of 175 hp. The installed engine (c/n 3) used a two cycle concept, with each of the four pairs of cylinders having a common combustion chamber. The engine was never produced and the project dropped. The C-165 (c/n 568, NX25463) was completed August 15, 1940 and first flown September 27. Tony LeVier, later a famous Lockheed test pilot, was the pilot for General Motors. The "GM Special" was painted Insignia Red with Diana Cream trim and Insignia blue pinstriping. Photo above shows late engine cowl installation. See original configuration page 101. Three C-165D airplanes were built (c/n 579, NC25484; 584, NC32451 and 586, NC32453) with a 175 hp Warner. There are no known photos.

T-50 (Prototype) ATC 772 1 built, 1939

Designed as a light twin selling for $30,000, Cessna's T-50 (c/n 1000, NX20784) took off for the first time on Sunday, March 26, 1939 with the company president Dwane Wallace at the controls for the 20-minute flight. The 5-place, low wing retractable was tested for over 100 hours and after modifications to bring it to production standards, it was sold to Pan American Airways and registered XA-BLU in Mexico. In June 1941 the same airplane was further modified with a new wing and fuselage appointments and at that time was assigned c/n 1000A. The prototype was powered with 2 Jacobs 225 hp engines with Curtiss-Reed fixed pitch propellers.

T-50 (Production) (UC-78A, D)　　　　　　　　　**ATC 772**　　　　　　　　　40*built, 1940-1942 *including prototype

Shown on December 6, 1939 is the final configuration of the first T-50 (c/n 1000). Modifications to production standard included a curved windscreen, different rear window shape, vertical tail shape and installation of Hamilton Standard constant speed propellers. The 2 Jacobs L4MB engines of 225 hp, were rated 245 hp for take-off. The T-50 was offered to the civilian market at $29,675. The CAA bought 8 of the first 19 built. In late 1940 production was terminated to switch to wartime production on the AT-8 and RCAF Crane I. In 1941 an additional 22 T-50's were produced for Pan American and the CAA. The 5-place 5100 lb gross T-50 had a service ceiling of 22,000 ft. There were 17 commercial T-50's impressed into service as UC-78A, those limited to 5300 lb gross became UC-78D.

T-50 Crane I　　　　　　　　　**RCAF Military**　　　　　　　　　640 built, 1940-1942

Cessna's largest production order to that date came for the 640 Crane I's ordered by the Canadian government in September 1940. Photo shows the 29th Crane I (c/n 1128, s/n 7685) on March 5,1941. The Canadian Crane I was powered by two 245 hp (military rating) Jacobs L4MB engines (normal take-off power was 225 hp) with most having fixed pitch wooden props; some later aircraft had metal fixed pitch props. Configuration was the same as the civil T-50 with the addition of cabin top windows, wooden props and other radio and instrumentation changes. Color overall was RCAF chrome yellow with black stenciling and letters, and standard Canadian roundels and fin flash. Performance and dimensions were identical to AT-8 except for a 195 mph top speed.

AT-8   U. S. Air Corps   33 built, 1941

Cessna's first military contract was for 33 AT-8 bomber-trainer airplanes built in 1941. The first one shown here (c/n 1030, Air Corps s/n 41-5) was delivered six months after contract signing. AT-8 differed from civil T-50 with cabin top windows, two Lycoming R-680, 9-cylinder radial engines with take-off 240 (225 normal) hp. Special radio equipment was installed along with Sperry hydraulic autopilots, and metal, constant speed props. The 33 AT-8 were c/n 1030-1062, AAF s/n 41-5 to 41-37. Wingspan was 41 ft 11-in., Length 31 ft 9-in. height 9 ft 11-in. Empty weight was 3500 lb with a gross of 5100. The AT-8 cruised at 175 mph (top 191) with a range of 750 miles and service ceiling of 22,000 ft.

AT-17 Bobcat (AT-17E)   U. S. Air Corps   450 built, 1942

In 1942 the Air Corps ordered 450 AT-17 Bobcats as advanced multi-engine and bomber pilot trainers. The first one built is shown above (c/n 1701, s/n 42-2). The five-place AT-17 had additional top windows and structural changes to the wing (after c/n 1763) to permit a gross weight of 5700 lbs instead of 5100 lbs. Structural problems with the main spar caused some AT-17 to be limited to 5300 lbs gross; these aircraft were re-designated AT-17E. Two Jacobs R-755-9 engines (245 take-off, 225 standard hp) were installed with two 2-bladed Hamilton Standard constant speed metal props. Dimensions and performance were the same as AT-8 except for 175 mph cruise (195 top) speed.

AT-17A and Crane Ia (AT-17C, D, F, UC-78C) U.S. Air Corps & RCAF **550 built, 1942**

Canadians ordered 550 Crane Ia airplanes but due to America's entry into World War II, only 182 were delivered to Canada. Illustrated is Crane Ia (c/n 2387, British s/n FJ186) in the Canadian training color of chrome yellow. AT-17A had the same R-755-9 engine of earlier AT-17, with additional top windows. Specifications and performance were also the same. Due to the wing structure problem, the AT-17A in use were re-designated AT-17F and limited to 5300 lbs gross. Deliveries were as follows (*see complete production data in appendix*) 182 AT-17A to Canada as Crane Ia; 41 to AAF as AT-17A; 60 to AAF as AT-17C; 131 to AAF as AT-17D (later UC-78C) and 136 to AAF as UC-78C. Designation differences dealt with military equipment and planned use - not changes in aircraft itself.

AT-17B Bobcat (AT-17G) U. S. Air Corps **466 built, 1942**

By now the Bobcat had been around long enough to pick up a few nicknames, including "Bamboo bomber" and "Double Breasted Cub". Photo shows AT-17B (c/n 3075 s/n 42-38866) in silver dope paint scheme and markings adopted May 15, 1942. Engines were Jacobs R-755-9 with either a Hamilton Standard constant speed metal prop or a Hartzell fixed pitch wooden one. Those AT-17B's limited to 5300 lbs gross weight were designated AT-17G. 655 AT-17B were ordered on Army contract W535-AC-20300 but the last 189 were changed from AT-17B to UC-78B before delivery. AT-17B military serials were 42-38692 to 42-39157 and Cessna c/n 2901 to 3366.

AT-17C Bobcat (AT-17H)   U. S. Air Corps   60 built, 1942

Originally ordered as a Crane Ia (AT-17A) for the RCAF under the Lend Lease program, the U. S. Air Corps took over the order prior to delivery - but as the above photo shows, not before some of the airplanes were painted. Above is AT-17C (c/n 2515, s/n 41-13831) with hand painted numbers on the tail and an RCAF roundel on the left wing. A number of AT-17C were redesignated AT-17H and operated with a lower maximum gross weight of 5300 lbs. Powerplant was the Jacobs R-755-9 driving Hartzell fixed pitch wooden props. Cessna c/n's were 2491 to 2550 with Air Corps s/n 42-13807 to 13866. Specifications and performance were the same as AT-17.

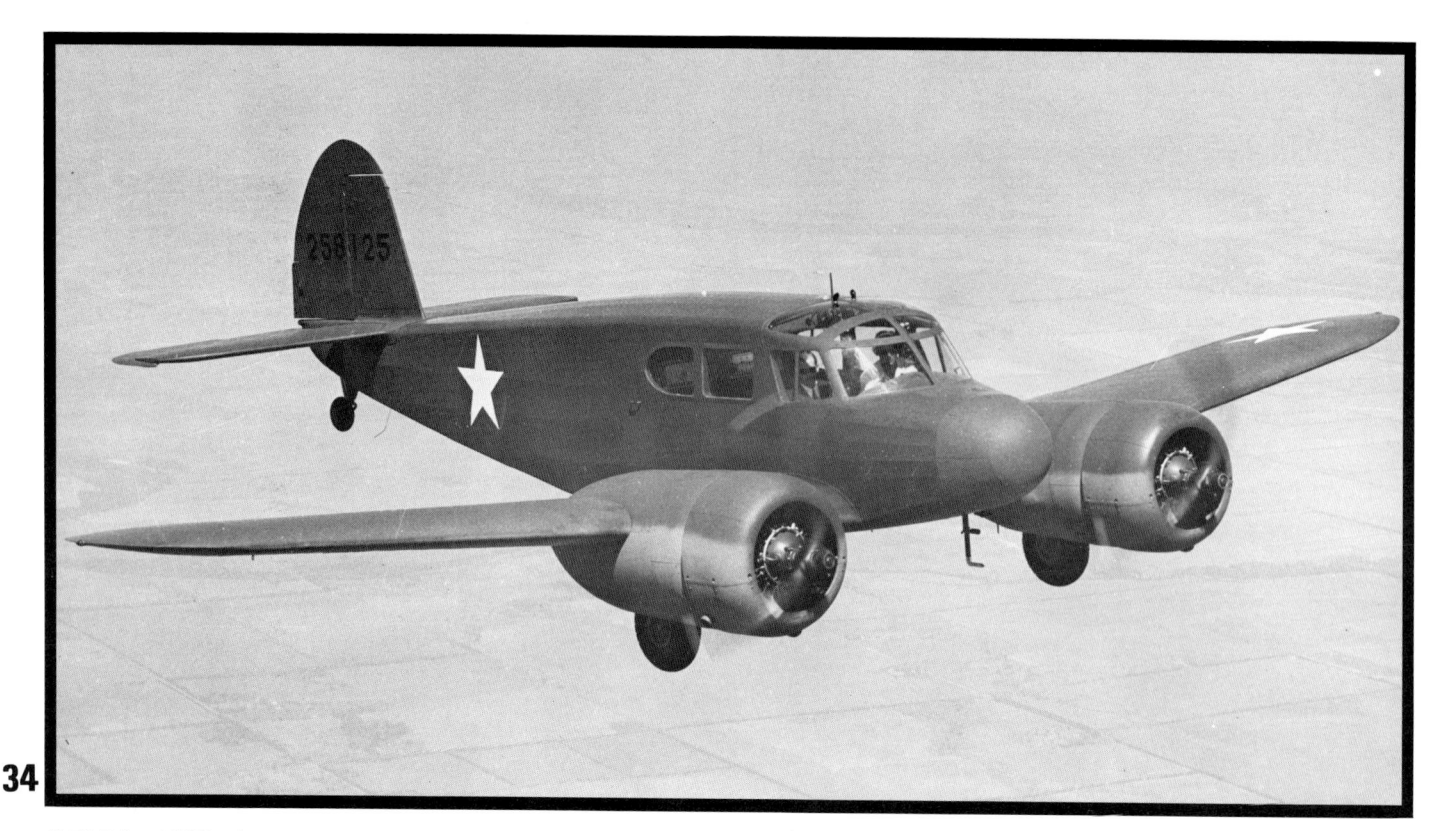

C-78 Bobcat (UC-78)   U. S. Air Corps   330 built, 1942-1944

A mission change to personnel transport and light cargo duties resulted in the "AT" series of Bobcats becoming the C-78 series. There were 330 airplanes delivered as C-78 and a further identical 674 airplanes as the UC-78, the only difference being a "paper" designation change adding the "U" for "utility" to the designation. Great in-flight shot of C-78 (c/n 3616, s/n 42-58125) shows position of main wheels when fully retracted. There were some radio and equipment changes from earlier models, and the C-78 was the first to receive the olive drab and gray paint scheme. Performance for the 5-place C-78 was the same as the earlier AT-17 except for the 5700 lb gross.

UC-78 Bobcat   **U. S. Air Corps**   **674 built, 1942-1944**

Photo of UC-78 (c/n 5042, s/n 43-7522) above was apparently taken shortly after July 1943. The red surrounding the national insignia was adopted in July 1943 and discarded two months later in September. Aircraft is overall olive drab with military s/n in yellow. The UC-78 was identical to the C-78, the only difference being a change in the designation to further reflect the role of the aircraft. There were 1004 C-78/UC-78 built; 67 of the UC-78 were transferred to the Navy as JRC-1. Rate of climb for all of the Bobcat types was 1325 fpm. Cruise 175 (top 195) with a 750 mile range and service ceiling of 22,000 ft. These statistics remained constant throughout production life of the Bobcats.

UC-78B Bobcat (UC-78E)   **U. S. Air Corps**   **2156 built, 1943-1944**

All UC-78B airplanes left the factory in the doped silver finish illustrated above by c/n 6107, s/n 43-32169. Photograph was prior to September 1943 as shown by the red around the national insignia. Those UC-78B aircraft limited to 5300 lbs were redesignated UC-78E. There were 2156 UC-78B built, Cessna c/n 3365-3555, 4161-4800 and 5374-6700. Powerplant was the Jacobs R-755-9. Some had wooden props of fixed pitch, others had constant speed metal props.

JRC-1 Bobcat   U. S. Navy   67 from AAF, 1942-1944

The U.S. Navy received 67 Air Corps UC-78 airplanes for "utility" flying roles. The Bobcat (also affectionatelly known as "Box kite") was received by the Navy in AAF markings, and the Navy paint schemes were applied over these. Some of the JRC-1 had two-tone blue and white, others a dark blue and white, still others were painted overall silver. Shown above is JRC-1 (BuAer No. 64456). BuAer numbers for the 67 Navy airplanes were 55772-55783 and 64442-64496. Engines were the Jacobs R-755-9 with Hamilton Standard constant speed metal props. Performance and specifications were as for the UC-78 with a 5700 lb max gross weight.

T-50 A   Experimental   1 built, 1941

The T-50A was a higher powered version of the T-50 series with plywood covered wing and tail surfaces instead of fabric. The fuselage was still fabric covered. All dimensions were identical to the T-50. Aircraft was manufactured on June 2, 1941. Shown in flight, the only T-50A (c/n P7, NX34750) was dismantled on October 14, 1942. Engines on the five-place airplane were two 300 hp Jacobs L-6MB engines.

P-10   **Experimental**   **1 built, 1941**

Using many Bobcat components, the Cessna P-10 was designed as a high performance two-place twin engine trainer (same class as Curtiss AT-9.) The only P-10 (c/n P-10, NX34751) was completed on October 4, 1941; first flight was on October 6. The Air Corps was not interested and the P-10 was dismantled a year later on October 14. Power was two Jacobs 300 hp-L6MB engines with two bladed Hamilton Standard constant speed metal props. Like the P-7, the P-10 had plywood covered wing and tail surfaces. Additionally, the fuselage was more slender than the T-50/P-7 and the wing span reduced. Except for the welded steel frame of the fuselage, the P-10 was built of non-strategic materials.

C-106   **Experimental**   **1 built, 1943**

Designed to provide a maximum cargo load and use a minimum of strategic war materials, the one C-106 (Cessna Engineering Project 260, c/n 1, NX 24176) was rolled out January 1943. The two-crew C-106 could carry 2440 lbs of cargo in 596 cubic feet of area. Fuselage was fabric covered steel tubing. Wings and tail surfaces were plywood covered. The only aluminum skin was around the cockpit and the engine nacelles. Control surfaces were fabric. U.S. insignia on the civilian airplane was due to a U. S. "letter of intent" for 500 airplanes. C-106 was scrapped before end of war, registration finally cancelled on January 6, 1948. Engines were two Pratt & Whitney R-1340, 600 take-off (550 normal) hp. Specifications in appendix.

C-106A Loadmaster Experimental 1 built, 1943

The C-106A was an improved version of the C-106, featuring full feathering 3-bladed Hamilton Standard props of 10-ft diameter; a geared Pratt & Whitney R-1340-AN2 engine of 600 take-off (550 normal) hp; a redesigned fuselage and cargo door and many equipment refinements. First flight of the only C-106A (c/n 10002, NX 44600) was April 9, 1943. An Air Corps letter of intent for 500 airplanes was received but due to low production priority enough materials could not be obtained to meet production schedules so the contract never materialized. The C-106A was scraped before the end of WWII. Specifications for both C-106 and C-106A were the same: Length 51 ft 2-in., span 64 ft 8-in., height 11 ft 4½-in., gross weight 14,000 lb and empty weight 9000 lbs.

120 ATC A-768 2172 built, 1946-1949

The two-place 120 was an economy version of the 140. The two types shared the same ATC number, the same production line, and their construction-numbers were comingled. The 120 did not have the wing flaps, additional side windows, or electrical system (except as an option) of the 140. However, at $2845 ($1500 less than the 140) the price was an attraction. Including the prototype which was completed December 1945, there were 2172 of the 120 built between June 1946 and May 1949. Dimensions and performance were similar to the 140 series; wingspan was 32 ft 10-in.; length 21 ft 6-in.; height 6 ft 3¼-in.; empty weight was 785 lbs (the 140 was 890). Performance showed a service ceiling of 15,500 ft and top speed of 120 mph. Engine was the C-85-12 of 85 hp.

140 (Prototype)   ATC A-768   3 built, 1945

Three prototypes for the postwar 140 were built (c/n 8000, 8001, 8002). The first, (c/n 8000, NX 41682) flew for the first time June 28, 1945, and was used to prove the airframe and flying characteristics of the all-new type. The second and third airplanes were refinements to production standard and differed in that they had a new engine cowl arrangement, an additional set of side windows and a redesigned tail cone. Shown above is (c/n 8000, NX41682) shortly after completion. The second and third airplanes were flown in the fall of 1945. The prototype 140 was the first Cessna to incorporate the later famous "spring steel" landing gear leg. The 140 prototypes were powered by the Continental C-85-12 engine.

140 (Production)   ATC A-768   4904 built, 1946-1949

Selling for $3385, the 140 was built as a low cost, all metal, two place trainer and sport airplane from May 1946 until April 1949, when it was succeeded by the 140A. Production of the 140 was on the same production line as the 120 series, and their c/n are comingled (c/n 8000 through 15075). The last 140 was c/n 15074. Total 140 production of 4904 includes the three prototypes. Engine of the 140 was the Continental C-85-12 of 85 hp until the 1948 model was introduced at which time the engine was the C-90-12. External appearance was the same. Photo shows c/n 9308 which was delivered July 31, 1946. The 140 had a fabric covered wing with metal flaps and ailerons. Wingspan was 32 ft 10-in.; length 21 ft 6-in.; top speed 120 (125 mph in 1948) and cruise speed 105 mph.

140A   ATC 5A2   525 built, 1949-1951

The 140A was a refined 140 series airplane incorporating an all metal wing replacing the "ragwing" of the 120/140 series. The first "all metal" Cessna, the 140A was offered with a choice of engines. The 85 hp Continental C-85-12 140A version sold for $3495 and there were 124 built. The 90 hp C-90-12 powered 140A sold for $3695 and there were 401 built. Production of the 140A included c/n 15200 through 15724 and was produced from May 1949 through March 1951. Sales of the 140A were sluggish due to the acceptance of the larger and faster 170. Shown is 140A (N5320C) with an optional 1950 style all-over paint scheme and optional wheel fairings. Top speed of the two-place 140A was 125 mph, cruise was 110 mph and it had a range of 500 miles with an endurance of 4 hours and 30 minutes. Empty weight was 900 lbs.

150 (1959 Model)   ATC 3A19   684 built

Cessna re-entered the two-place trainer market in 1959 with the Model 150. Designed to replace the out-of-production 120/140 series, the prototype (c/n 617, N34258) was built as the Model 142 and licensed Oct 10, 1957. This was changed to Model 150 on October 16. Registration was cancelled Nov 21, 1960 and the aircraft dismantled. Production 150's featured Cessna's high lift flaps, tricycle landing gear and all metal construction. Engine was a 100 hp Continental 0-200-A. The 150 was sold in three versions, increasing in options and price. They were Standard at $6995, Trainer at $7940 and Commuter at $8545. Shown above is the first production 150 (c/n 17001, N5501E) in standard paint styling, with the optional wheel fairings. The 1959 model included the prototype built in 1957 and 683 production airplanes (c/n 17001 through 17683.)

150 (1960 Model) ATC 3A19 334 built

No major changes were incorporated in the 1960 production 150 series. Refinements included reducing prop diameter from 6 ft 2-in. to 5 ft 9-in., and a heated pitot tube and a stall warning horn were now offered to permit use as an instrument trainer. Shown above is a Patroller version (c/n 17720, N7920E) which had such non-standard appointments as the door panels with additional window area, a message chute on the left side of the cabin in front of pilot's seat, and a 35 gallon fuel capacity giving a 980 mile range (630 miles was the basic 150 range). CAP aircraft above was in non-standard paint of white, with black trim and orange day-glo panels. The 1960 production 150's were c/n 17684 through 17999 and 59001 through 59018. Engine was the 100 hp Continental 0-200-A. Base price of all versions was increased about $200.

150A (1961 Model) ATC 3A19 333 built

First external changes were made in the 150A of 1961. Shown above is the prototype 150A (c/n 628, N34268) which shows the large rear cabin window. The main landing gear was redesigned to move the wheels 2-in. aft, shifting the CG further forward. Other changes included reduction of empty weight by 12 lb (increasing the useful load by the same weight) and design of a new instrument panel into a "Y" configuration for flight instruments. Engine was the 100 hp Continental 0-200-A. The 333 airplanes of the 1961 model year included the prototype (c/n 628) and 332 production airplanes c/n 15059019 through 15059350. Dimensions were the same as earlier versions: Wingspan 33 ft 4-in.; Length 22 ft 11-in.; Height 6 ft 11-in. without beacon and 7 ft 1½-in. with beacon. Top speed remained at 124 mph and cruise was 121.

150B (1962 Model) ATC 3A19 350 built

Over 1700 150's were sold during the first four years of production (1959 through 1962). The 150B had a redesigned wingtip fairing which was identical to that used on most other Cessna single engine airplanes, and which enclosed the wingtip light. Overall length was increased 1-in. to 33 ft 6-in. due to larger, more pointed fiberglass spinner instead of aluminum one. Top speed was increased to 127 mph and cruise speed to 125 mph with addition of a new McCauley propeller. The 350 airplanes of the 1962 series Model 150B were c/n 15059351 through 15059700. In 1962 the Commuter version was selling for $8995. Range for the 150B was 610 miles and the service ceiling 15,600 ft.

150C (1963 Model) ATC 3A19 387 built

Further refinements on the 150C included a redesign of the instrument panel to improve lighting and to reduce glare for night flying. The optional wheel fairings were redesigned to be interchangeable with the rest of the single Cessna airplanes. The 387 1963 series 150C airplanes were c/n 15059701 through 15060087. Engine was the Continental 0-200-A. Cruise of the 150C was 125 mph at 75 percent power at 7500 ft. Baggage allowance was 80 lb, and a couple of small "bucket seats" for kids was an option. Fuel capacity was 26 gallons and the "no reserve" range was 5.9 hours using 22.5 gallons. The Commuter sold for $9435. Service Ceiling was 15,600 ft.

150D (1964 Model) ATC 3A19 686 built

Omni-vision came to the 150D in 1964. The rear fuselage decking was reduced to provide wrap-around 360° vision. Gross weight was up 100 lbs (to 1600 lbs) with 40 lbs of this as additional useful load. This eased a problem of additional avionics being added to the airplanes. Photo shows the 150D prototype (c/n 644, N5420E). Base price of the Commuter increased slightly to $9495. While dimensions of the 150D remained the same, the introduction of the wrap-around windows drastically changed its appearance, and while most performance figures were similar, with a top speed of 125 mph, a cruise of 122, a range of 565 miles and initial rate of climb was 670 fpm, the service ceiling was lower at 12,650 ft.

150E (1965 Model) ATC 3A19 760 built

Minor design refinements and the annual paint scheme change were about all of the changes in the 1965 Model 150E. Shown in flight is the first 150E (c/n 15060773, N6073T). There were 760 of the 1965 Model 150E with the c/n 15060773 through 15061532. Engine was the Continental 0-200-A of 100 hp. Cruise speed was 122 mph for the two-place (four place with "family seating" bucket seats). Commuter price was less than previous years at $9425.

150F (1966 Model)　　　　　　　　　　**ATC 3A19**　　　　　　　　　　**3001 built**

The 3001 production run of the 150F of 1966 included one prototype (c/n 649, N5423E shown above), 2933 produced in the USA, and 67 produced as the F150F by Cessna's French affiliate Reims Aviation. The first airplanes in France were produced from assemblies in Wichita. Later airplanes were completely built in France, and were powered by the Rolls Royce version of the Continental 0-200-A. 1966 c/n's were 15061533 through 15064532. The 67 airplanes assembled in France also were assigned c/n's which were F1500001 through F1500067. The two place 150F wingspan was 9½-in. less than the 150E, and the length increased by 21-in. due to the 35° swept back tail assembly. New 6.00 x 6 wheels, tires and brakes (interchangable with the 172 airplanes) replaced the previous 5.00 x 5 assembly. Commuter price was $9275.

150G (1967 Model)　　　　　　　　　　**ATC 3A19**　　　　　　　　　　**2818 built**

The 150G prototype (c/n 649, N3763C) was actually the 150F prototype modified into the first 150G of 1967, re-numbered and put on floats. The 2818 150G airplanes included 2666 produced in the USA (c/n 15064533 through 15067198) and 152 French airplanes (c/n F150068 through F1500219.) Change included a new instrument panel and cowl deck. Fuselage contour was changed to provide additional cabin width in the area of the doors. Foot and leg room was increased by deepening the floorboard aft of the rudder pedals. Cowling was isolated from the airframe by 8 shockmounts on brackets to reduce vibration. Engine was the 100 hp Continental 0-200-A, and the French F150G had the Rolls Royce 0-200-A version. Floatplane had top speed of 102 mph, cruise of 98 and service ceiling of 10,700 ft. Commuter sold for $9550.

150H (1968 Model)   ATC 3A19   2280 built

In the fall of 1967, production of the 150 airplanes was transferred to Strother Field, between Winfield and Arkansas City, Kansas. C/n 15067659 was the first 150H produced there. Shown above is the 10,000th 150 built, c/n 15068075, N22124, a 1968 150H Commuter. Dimensions and performance were identical to the 150G of 1967. Refinements included availability of a Brittain wing leveler, a pneumatically operated two axis automatic control system. The 2280 150H models included 2110 (c/n 15067199 through 15069308) produced in the USA and 170 of the F150H (c/n F1500220 through F1500389) produced in France. Engine models were the same. Price of the 2-place Commuter was $10,195. Wingspan was 32 ft 8 ½-in., length 23 ft 9-in. and the empty weight was 1060 lbs. Top speed was 122 mph and cruise was 117 mph.

150J (1969 Model)   ATC 3A19   1960 built

The 150J (there was no 150I) was another "refined" version. Primary changes included an all-new instrument panel, additional leg room, and re-designed wheel fairings. Overhaul time on the Continental 100 hp 0-200-A engine was increased to 1800 hours. Photo shows 150J (c/n 15069367 with Venezuelan registration YV-T-CTU) in standard marking. 150 production transferred back to the Wichita Pawnee plant after the last 150J during the belt-tightening days of the "recession." Production included 1820 (c/n 15069309 through 15071128) USA airplanes and 140 of the French F150J (c/n F1500390 through F1500529). Comuter price was $10,995. Performance and specifications were similar to the earlier models; rate of climb was 670 fpm, service ceiling was 12,650 feet and the maximum range was 565 miles.

150K (1970 Model) ATC 3A19 1004 built

Production of the 150K was at the Pawnee Plant of Cessna, following the closing of the Strother Field facility. Beginning with the 150K, the Commuter version was equipped with conical camber wing tips, adding 5½-in. to the wingspan. Standard and trainer wingspan was 32 ft 8½-in., the Commuter was 33 ft 2-in. Other dimensions were the same as previous years. Changes included a molded headliner replacing fabric; the overhead console was redesigned to allow installation of optional skylights and easier maintenance; and seats were redesigned to give still more leg room. Production included 875 USA produced airplanes (c/n 15071129 through 15072003) and 129 French airplanes (c/n F1500530 through F1500658). Engine was either Continental or Rolls Royce 0-200-A depending on factory location. The Commuter sold for $11,450.

A150K Aerobat (1970 Model) ATC 3A19 307 built

Designed for limited aerobatics, the A150K was the first Cessna built specifically for this purpose. Price was $10,495. The airframe structure was strengthened to meet CAR Part 3; changes included capability of +6G/-3G flight loads; quick release cabin doors; shoulder harnesses; "G" meter; and a special paint scheme. Overhead skylights were standard on the Aerobat (they were an option on other versions). Aircraft was approved for barrel and aileron rolls, single snaps, loops, immelmans, cuban eights, spins and vertical reversements. Inverted flight manuevers were not permitted. Wingspan was 33 ft 2-in.; other dimensions and performance figures the same as other versions. There were 226 A150K produced in the USA (c/n A1500001 through A1500226) and 81 French produced FA150K (c/n FA150001 through FA150081).

150L (1971 through 1973 Models)   ATC 3A19   3202 built

The 150 had been refined to such a degree by 1971 that the model number was not changed although a different paint scheme and minor styling differences were given each model year airplane. Production follows: 625 in 1971; 1030 in 1972; and 1192 in 1973 (c/n 15072004 through 15074850). The 150L is being produced in 1974. French production of the F150L was 80 in 1971; 125 in 1972; and 150 in 1973 (c/n F1500659 through F1501013). The overall height of the 150L was reduced 7½-in. (to 7 ft 9½-in.) due to a switch from spring steel landing gear to a tubular steel assembly. This gave a smoother ride on the ground, absorbed landing shocks better and saved 18 lbs. Landing light was moved to the nose cap and a longer dorsal fin improved stability. Commuter price was $11,995 in 1971; $12,550 in 1972-1974.

A150L Aerobat (1971 through 1973 Models)   ATC 3A19   333 built

Shown in all its glory is a 1973 Aerobat A150L (c/n A1500343, N6043J). Paint and styling changes were primary differences between the 1971 through 1974 Aerobat models. As with 150L models, the A150L had the tubular steel landing gear assembly; the landing light on the nose cap and a longer dorsal fin. First engine change in the history of the 150 series came with the addition of a Rolls Royce 130 hp 0-240-A on the FRA150L built in France starting in 1972. The A150L (USA) and the FA150L had the Continental/Rolls Royce 0-200-A 100 hp engine. Production figures follow: 50 of the A150L in 1971; 66 in 1972 and 87 in 1973 (c/n A1500227 through A1500429). French production was 39 FA150L in 1971; 46 FRA150L in 1972 and 45 FRA150L in 1973 (c/n FA1500082 through FA1500120; FRA1500121 through FRA1500211).

150L (1974 Model)   **3A19**   **576 (1974)**

The Cessna 150L of 1974 is a further refined model of the most popular training/sport airplane ever produced. During the 1974 model year production exceeded 19,600 airplanes built since the 150 was first introduced in 1959. The 1974 150L was produced in four versions, Standard (955 lbs empty); Trainer (1015 lbs empty); Commuter (1060 lbs empty); and Aerobat (see below). The Commuter base price was $12,550 and all other 150 models remained the same price as in 1972. The 150L was produced in France as the F150L. There were no Argentine A-150L produced in 1974, however there were 18 built in 1972, 15 in 1973 and 5 in 1975. Initial production c/n for the 1974 150L was 15074851 and in France it was F1501014. Refinements include interior, wheel fairings and exterior styling. Statistically the 1974 150L is identical with earlier models. Wingspan is 33 ft 2-in. (Commuter) and 32 ft 8½-in. (all other versions), length is 23 ft 9-in, and height is 7 ft 9½-in. or 8 ft with beacon.

A150L Aerobat (1974 Model)   **3A19**   **85 USA, 14 France, 1974 Model Year**

The 1974 A150L Aerobat has a higher top speed, cruise speed and service ceiling, and is available at the same price as a comparable 1972 Aerobat. The new "Clark Y" airfoil propeller installation has provided a speed increase of 4 mph (top 124, cruise 119 at 75% power at 7000 ft) and the service ceiling is up 1350 ft to 14,000 ft. Like the basic 1974 150L models, the Aerobat has been further refined in detail; including interior appointments, exterior styling and wheel fairings. Production of the 1974 A150L begins with c/n A1500430, and in France the FRA150L starts with c/n FRA1500212. Engine on the American A150L is the Continental 0-200-A of 100 hp at 2750 rpm. FRA150L engine is the Rolls Royce (Continental) 0-240-A of 130 hp. The two-place Aerobat has a maximum gross weight of 1600 lbs, and an empty weight of 1040 lbs. Rate of climb (SL) is 670 fpm. Stall is 55 mph (flaps up, power off) and 48 mph (flaps down, power off).

150M (1975 Model)　　　　　　　　　　**3A19**　　　　　　　　　　**1224 USA, 105 France**

An aerodynamic clean-up which started with the Aerobat in 1974 was extended to the 150M in 1975. This gave the 150M 21.8 mpg at maximum recommended cruise speeds, which in themselves were three mph faster than the earlier 150L. Increased fin and rudder area improved cross wind landing capabilities and a more efficient propeller and drag reductions due to redesigned wheel and brake fairings also resulted in a more efficient aircraft. Price for the standard 150M was $10,700, the Commuter $14,250 and the Commuter II $16,925. Commuter II designation made a fourth basic model available and featured the most commonly ordered options as "standard" which resulted in saving almost $2500 if these options were ordered separately. Production of the 150M started with c/n 15075782-15077005 and in France as the F150M with F15001144-F15001248. See page 104 for performance and specifications.

A150M (1975 Model) Aerobat　　　　　　**3A19**　　　　　　**86 USA, 20 France, 1975 model**

A distinctive paint scheme and certification for aerobatic maneuvers of 6 G positive and 3 G negative flight load factors and maneuvers such as barrel rolls, aileron rolls, spins, loops and vertical reversements were features of the Aerobat series. Quick release doors, and provisions for parachute seat packs and other aerobatic equipment were additional Aerobat features. Powered by the 100 hp Continental O-200A the 1975 A150M sold for $13,325. There were 20 1975 FRA150M produced in France with a Rolls Royce O-240A of 130 hp. Empty weight of the A150M was 1040 lbs and it had a service ceiling of 14,000 ft, a range of 650 miles and a top speed of 124 mph.

150M (1976 Model) 3A19 **Current production**

Redesigned wheel fairings on the Commuter II 150M gave it a 2 mph speed advantage over the standard 150M of 1976. Production of the 1976 150M series started with c/n 15077006 and there were four versions, Standard selling for $12,650, Commuter at $16,350, Commuter II at $18,750 and Aerobat (described in next paragraph). In France 1976 F150M production started with F 15001249. Very minor refinements and a new paint scheme were main differences in 1975 and 1976 models of the 150M series.

A150M (1976 Model) 3A19 **Current production**

Added rudder area to the 1975-1976 150M and A150M series added 2½-in. to overall length and 6-in. to height and gave more response in flight and in crosswind landings and take-offs. Like the 150M models, the 1976 A150M had a new paint scheme and other refinements but was essentially the same as the 1975 model. Price of the Aerobat in 1976 was $15,250. Produced in France, the FRA150M had a 130 hp Rolls Royce O-240A while the USA A150M featured the Continental O-200A. All Aerobat versions featured quick release doors and other aerobatic essentials. G loads were 6 positive and 3 negative.

"A Master's Expression"

A PORTFOLIO OF HISTORIC CESSNA INFORMATION

At a certain time and at a certain place, the advertising and editorial presented on the following pages was current news. It was the latest information about a new airplane. It was alive.

It was important to Cessna because it told the public about their airplanes and their achievements. It was also important because people were told what they needed to know about the airplanes they might want to buy, or to fly. These truths are just as important today in the mod-70's as they were in the 20's or 30's.

Years after the fact, the information now old, outmoded and out of style, takes on new meaning. It tells us today, what was important, "back then." It conveys a feeling of that certain time; that special time which was once, but is nevermore. It brings back our past. Read the following pages like they are today and see for yourself.

Cessna Aircraft Company
ENCLOSED CANTILEVER MONOPLANES

WICHITA, KANS

Cessna On The Salt Plains Ready for a Try-out

Everything Ready and Will Fly as Soon as Weather is Favorable——May be Here Three Weeks

Lindsley Bi-Monoplane Coming Tomorrow

C. V. Cessna, of Enid, is now on the southwestern edge of the Great Salt Plains ready to start his flying machine. The windy weather has delayed him several days but with such nice weather as this of today he will be able to start soon.

The machine is of French make, Bleroit pattern, equipped with an American motor, 80 h.p. It is strongly built but of very light material and weighs about 800 pounds. It is about 40 feet long and the wings measure about 18 feet, tip to tip. It appears like a huge bird at a distance. It is no experiment; the machine will fly without any doubt whatever.

Mr. Cessna has never driven this nor any other machine, but has many times accompanied others in flights. His purpose here is to learn machine and prepare to enter meets. He says he is positive he can go up "but when it comes to lighting, that's the hard proposition, and that's why I came here. This is an ideal place; nothing to interfere with the machine in any way. It may take me three weeks before I am satisfied" said Mr. Cessna.

Many are going to see the machine and asking as to when he will fly, etc. but no date was set. It all depends on the weather. He gave us a thorough description of the machine and the work performed by the different parts, and this being our first visit to one of these machines, it was certainly appreciated.

The Bi-monoplane belonging to Mr. Lindsley, father of Ed Lindsley, is expected to arrive tomorrow and it will be given a try-out by Mr. Cessna

We hope to be able to tell of several successful flights with each machine next week.

AVIATOR FALLS WITHOUT INJURY

Jet, Okla., Sept. 15.—While trying out his machine Thursday afternoon, C. V. Cessna, who has been out on the Salt Plains five miles northwest of this place, met with an accident which will delay his practice for several days.

After a flight of about a mile and a half, he turned to complete his trip and the machine turned turtle, smashing the front part of the machine. Both wings crumpled into a useless heap. The aviator escaped with but slight bruises, after rolling a distance of thirty feet.

For several weeks he has been at this place practicing and had just about decided to accept some date to do exhibition work, but his accident will delay him for several weeks.

Cessna Made Successful Flight

C. V. Cessna, the Enid aviator, made a successful five-mile flight at Enid last Sunday afternoon. His Bleriot monoplane, the one he used here in his practice flights on the Salt Plains, had been repaired and hardly showed signs of the wrecked condition in which it left here.

Cessna flew a distance of five miles in seven minutes, reaching a height of 200 feet. The many friends the aviator made during his stay here will be glad to learn of his success.

AIRSHIP CRIED THE FAIR CROWD

And During Exciting Race Rago Aviator Flew Over the Grand Stand.

The 2:30 trot was just about to experience a close finish—the crowd was getting itself strung up to the right pitch—someone who happened to have his eye off the horses for a moment jumped right straight up in the middle of the stand and shouted "an airship". Then the whir of a propeller was heard. Three or four thousand pairs of eyes gave up the race and centered them upon an object coming 500 feet high over the field. It was a real airship—big as life.

C. V. Cessna, a farmer aviator of Rago, had come down to visit the fair. Had never seen the Anthony fair, he said, and just ran down a few moments to see what it looked like. A few of the fair directors got their heads together and told Mr. Cessna that for another little flight and one on Friday they would give him a cold hundred and he said he was on. Hence it was that on Friday the fair visitors saw one of the prettiest flights they ever did or will see. Mr. Cessna is a good sport and gave the crowd its money's worth. He flew home on Friday afternoon—after his exhibition.

This flight was an "extra" for which neither the fair association or the people had counted and added to the other attractions gave the people good measure for their tickets.

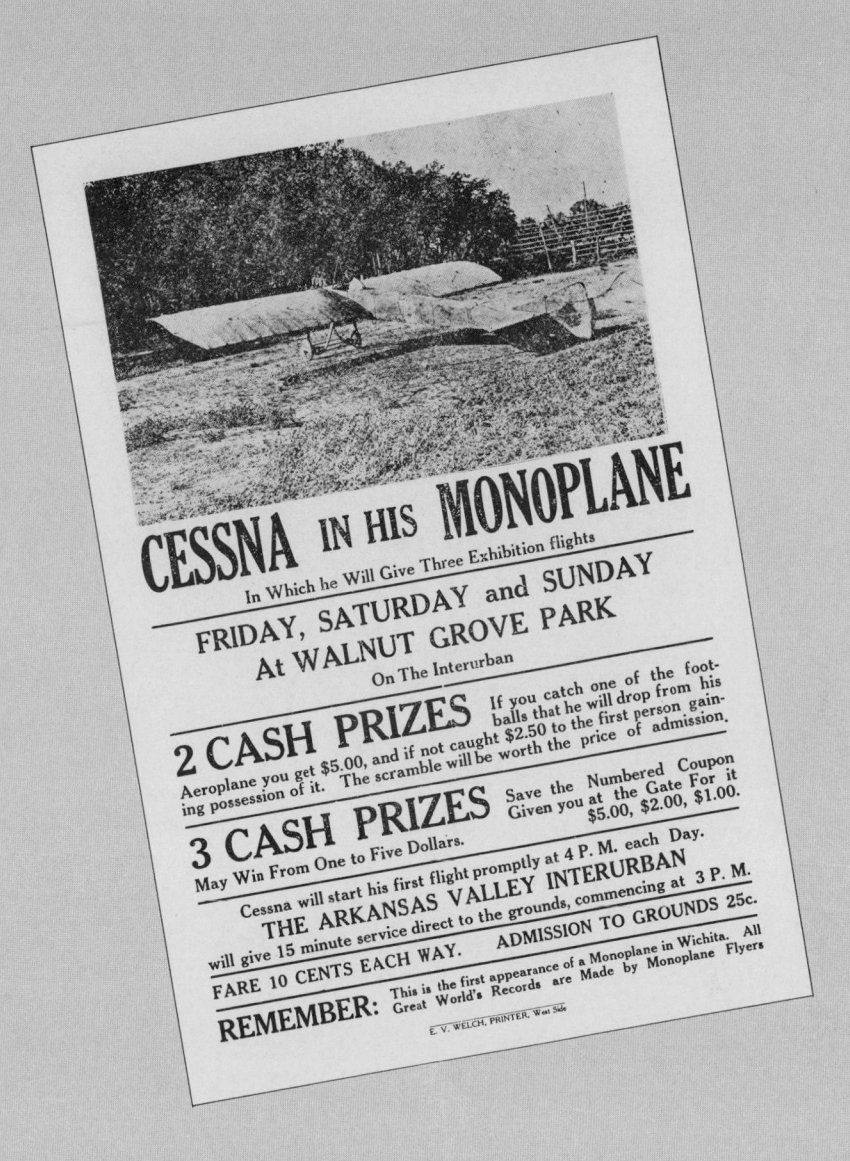

CESSNA IN HIS MONOPLANE
In Which he Will Give Three Exhibition flights

FRIDAY, SATURDAY and SUNDAY
At WALNUT GROVE PARK
On The Interurban

2 CASH PRIZES If you catch one of the footballs that he will drop from his Aeroplane you get $5.00, and if not caught $2.50 to the first person gaining possession of it. The scramble will be worth the price of admission.

3 CASH PRIZES Save the Numbered Coupon Given you at the Gate For it $5.00, $2.00, $1.00.
May Win From One to Five Dollars.

Cessna will start his first flight promptly at 4 P. M. each Day.
THE ARKANSAS VALLEY INTERURBAN will give 15 minute service direct to the grounds, commencing at 3 P. M.
FARE 10 CENTS EACH WAY.   ADMISSION TO GROUNDS 25c.

REMEMBER: This is the first appearance of a Monoplane in Wichita. All Great World's Records are Made by Monoplane Flyers

E. V. WELCH, PRINTER, West Side

LIKE A SCARED RABBIT

Cessna Flew Home in Eighteen Minutes and Went Slow, He Says.

We have a letter from C. V. Cessna, who did the aviating stunt at the fair. The letter was written the morning after Mr. Cessna flew home, and in part follows:

I had a very nice trip home, after leaving Anthony last evening, and made the trip in just eighteen minutes and could have made it in much less time, but allowed my motor to work very leisurely, as I was not in any particular hurry to get home, only in time for supper. My wife was expecting me home for supper and I was very comfortably enjoying the same with her at 6:30, having made the twenty-eight miles home and put the machine in the hangar in just twenty-five minutes after I took my seat at Anthony. That isn't bad, is it?

C. V. CESSNA.

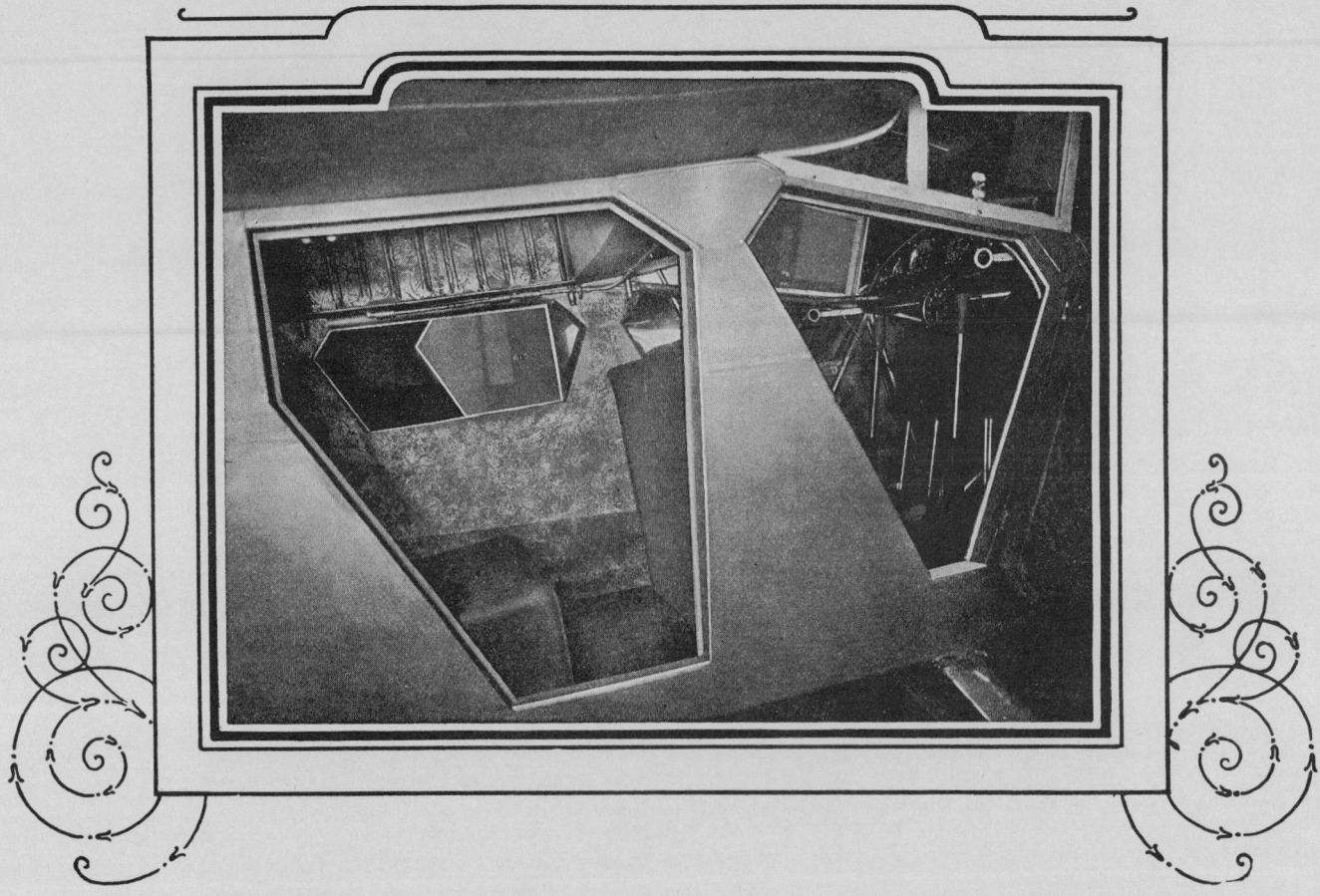

Closed Cars of the Air
Moderately Priced

CESSNA Cantilever Cabin Monoplanes offer the first complete 3 and 4-place cabin planes at moderate prices.

Beginning at $4700 for the 3-place ship, powered with a 120 H.P. Anzani motor, to the 4-place ship powered with a 200 H.P. Wright Whirlwind at $8980, these ships fill a market hitherto untouched.

In performance they are unequalled. Take off in 76 feet, climb to 1,000 feet in 26 seconds,—where can you match it? The Whirlwind motored Cessna ship recently flew from Wichita to Tulsa and return (150 air miles each way) making one lap in 1:05 and the return trip in one hour flat.

THIS MEANS GREATER SALES FOR DEALERS

Think what this complete line of moderately priced Cessna Cantilever Cabin Monoplanes means to the dealer who wants the cream of the business! Where can you find a 4-place cabin plane, powered with the famous 200 H.P. Wright Whirlwind to compare with the Cessna at anywhere near our price of $8980?

The trend is towards the closed ship —Cessna alone gives you the opportunity to fill this great and fast-growing market.

Want full details of our valuable dealer franchise? Write or wire today—your territory may still be open.

CESSNA AIRCRAFT COMPANY
WICHITA, KANSAS

SPEED

BECAUSE ITS AIR RESISTENCE IS LESS

GALILEO

Galileo first told the world, in 1590, why a stone drops faster than a feather — because its air-resistance is less in proportion to its bulk.

PICK whatever power plant you will, Ryan-Siemens, Comet, Floco, or 200 H.P. Wright Whirlwind, and the Cessna Cantilever Cabin Monoplane will out-fly and out-perform any other cabin plane, Horse-Power for Horse-Power.

Just as the rock falls past the floundering feather, so a Cessna Monoplane, under actual test, will leave behind any other cabin plane of equal horse-power on the market today.

The reason is simple. Cessna builds a plane that slips through the air with unequaled ease. Graceful, specially constructed Cantilever wings, minus the usual struts and braces — slender, compact body, stream-lined throughout — all parts of the Cessna combine to reduce wind-resistance, the great foe of plane speed, to a minimum.

Cessna has not sacrificed one iota of sturdiness, safety, or comfort, either. A glance at the specifications will make this evident.

Send for complete literature and dealer's proposition today. You will find them both more than interesting.

CESSNA

Clyde V. Cessna, first making use of this simple principle in building aircraft, gave the world a plane that is unrivaled in speed — *because its air-resistance is less.*

Cessna Aircraft Company
WICHITA, KANSAS

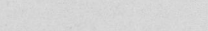

1928

SAFETY

MONOPLANES CESSNA

They're Both
CANTILEVER

The cantilever bridge—graceful, yet stupendously strong—supports its trundling burdens across the gaping abyss, in perfect Safety.

Above—on cantilever wings, speeds the Monoplane Cessna to its distant port—also in Snug Safety. Trim and trustworthy—both bridge and plane are outstanding examples of advanced engineering design ... marked achievements that inherit their great strength and safety from cantilever construction.

Cantilever wing design of Monoplanes Cessna eliminates all external bracing. Wind resistance is reduced to a minimum. Greater speed per horsepower is the result. Smart trimness contributes to unmatched performance.

Write or wire our Sales Representative for literature on Monoplanes Cessna.

CESSNA
"A MASTER'S EXPRESSION"

MANUFACTURED BY THE CESSNA AIRCRAFT CO., WICHITA, U. S. A.

CURTISS FLYING SERVICE, INC.
Sole Sales Agents for United States and Canada
GARDEN CITY, NEW YORK

1929

PERFORMANCE no. 1

which proved the rugged strength of the new Cessnas

Altitude 5000 feet . . . at that height a Cessna Test Pilot suddenly turned the nose of a new Cessna Monoplane downward—and an unusual test for stability began.

In a wild power dive, with throttle wide open, the new Cessna roared earthward—down, down, plunging 2000 feet—then into a quick zooming climb. . . . How fast, that power dive? 350 miles per hour—and the new Cessna never flinched, showed no sign of any weakness! Tested strength is built into every feature of the new Cessna Monoplanes. Notice in the picture below and at right the famous Cessna Cantilever Wing which withstands a weight of 15,752 lbs. with no ruptures or breaks of any kind. . . . Every Cessna owner appreciates the super-strength in the new Cessna Monoplanes—enjoys the assurance that when rough conditions do arise his plane will meet them safely. Once you take off in a new Cessna, a feeling of security envelops you. You have confidence in the staunch construction and the rugged strength of these modern planes. This fact coupled with the advantages of their mile-devouring speed assures a safe flight, a swift flight and a pleasant flight.

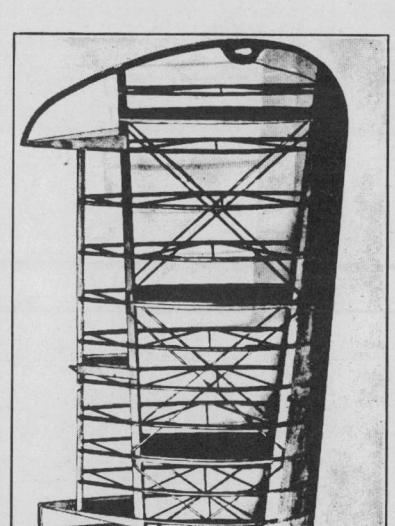

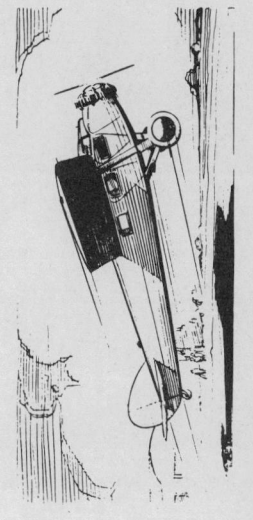

PERFORMANCE no. 2

in which the new Cessnas surprise many of the air-minded

Speed was expected in the new Cessna Monoplanes. Everyone throughout the entire field of aviation knew that the famous Cessna speed was too important an advantage to be lost in the new Cessna models . . . But only a few believed that this speed could be brought under such absolute control as it is in these new, easily operated monoplanes.

Actual figures in black and white taken in the beginning of the 1929 National Air Tour prove a mighty important advantage in the new Cessna Monoplanes. The combined stick and unstick time (landing speed and distance required for take-off) of each of the New Cessnas was less than that of any of the competing Monoplanes in the Tour . . . . All of which goes to prove that the New Cessnas can land and take off in a smaller field than the great majority of other monoplanes now in operation. A big advantage to the owner of a new Cessna—this ability to land easily and take-off quickly. In fact, it's a feature that every prospective airplane purchaser will soon demand in the plane he buys. Safety, of course, will always be the most important feature in an airplane; next in importance is speed—controlled speed—like that incorporated in the New Cessna Monoplanes. Step by step Cessna Monoplanes have been improved and refined until in the new models, DC-6A and DC-6B, they have advanced to a stage equalled by few other monoplanes. In safety, speed and ease of operation they are excelled by none. Horsepower for horsepower, the new Cessna Monoplanes will outfly any other plane in their class.

PERFORMANCE no. 3

with facts that will appeal to prospective Cessna owners

On April 5th, 1929, a Cessna Monoplane, after a remarkable performance, landed on Cessna Field. It had just completed a round trip from Wichita to Nome, Alaska—a journey of 13,085 miles, or more than half the distance around the world. All kinds of flying weather were encountered; but the Cessna made the journey in 127 hours, and its only maintenance was *one spark plug cleaned and one valve clearance adjusted.*

Now, the airplane has passed the novelty stage; today it is becoming a very necessary medium of transportation because it moves passengers, from place to place much faster than they could ever go before. Speed, safety, and now *economy*—these are all necessary features in the modern airplane.

New Cessna Monoplanes have proved that they will give you swift flight, safe flight, and *economical flight.* These new, trimly built, highly streamlined monoplanes operate with a combined fuel and oil cost of less than three cents per mile. They are equipped with comfortable reclining seats, interiors are finished with attractive upholstery. . . . In every way a new Cessna provides ideal transportation for the business executive, for airlines, and for private owners.

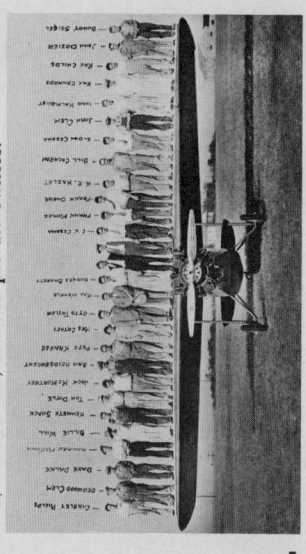

CESSNA AIRCRAFT COMPANY

WICHITA, KANSAS

CESSNA'S New Creation

The Speediest 6-place Transport behind ANY Motor

To be announced Dec. 1st.
See it at the
CHICAGO SHOW

The Cessna Aircraft Co.
Wichita, Kansas

The Sensation of the Chicago Show

The New 6-Place Cessna Transport

From Wichita to Chicago 730 Air Miles in 5 Hours 52 Minutes with the J-5 Wright Whirlwind Averaging 1600 R.P.M. Carrying 1150 Pounds Pay Load Passengers and Baggage

The center of admiration at the Chicago Show for its beauty and graceful lines — this new 6-place Cessna Cantilever Cabin Monoplane is just as sensational in Speed, Stability and Safety.

Its performance on its maiden trip from Wichita to Chicago, given at the left, once more proves the superior craftsmanship of its pioneer designer, Clyde V. Cessna.

Detailed specifications and prices will be gladly furnished upon request.

The Cessna Aircraft Co.
Wichita, Kansas

1929

Cessna's New Creation

Built with the same fine engineering principles which have brought the Cessna 4-place Cantilever Cabin Monoplane so many notable victories, this new 6-place Transport established a name for itself on its maiden flight from Wichita to Chicago.

With its Whirlwind motor averaging but 1600 R.P.M.s it carried a pay-load of 1150 pounds, passengers and baggage, at an average speed of 121 miles per hour over the entire trip—730 air miles.

With the new J-6, 300 H.P., for which it is built it should easily cruise at an average speed of 110 to 115 M.P.H.

Let us tell you more about these fine cruisers of the air—a request on your letterhead will bring full details.

The Cessna Aircraft Co.
Wichita, Kansas

PERFORMANCE

When you take the controls of your Cessna for the first time—and quickly leave the rest behind—then you'll really appreciate that extra 10 to 20 miles per hour that 18 years of constant development and experiment have enabled Clyde V. Cessna, Pioneer Designer, to give you in

MONOPLANES CESSNA

CESSNA
"A MASTER'S EXPRESSION"

CESSNA AIRCRAFT COMPANY
WICHITA, U.S.A.

1929

KANSAS to NEW YORK VIA SIBERIA

10,000-mile amazing WARNER-SCARAB performance

One month to the day, on which he left Detroit, Parker D Cramer was again in that city after the amazing 10,000 mile flight of his Warner-Scarab to Siberia.

Using the same plane and the same engine (No. 26) with which Earl Rowland won the New York to Los Angeles Air Derby last September, and flying 1400 miles a day when necessary, Cramer made the trip in 118 flying hours with only the slight adjustments to the engine mentioned in the telegram herein reproduced. And the return flight, Nome to New York, was made in 46 hours flying time.

During the flight all climatic conditions were encountered, beginning with the almost mid-summer temperature in Kansas, the starting point, through the balmy spring air of Alberta and into the zero weather of Alaska and Siberia.

Considered from every viewpoint this most recent Warner-Scarab performance is a magnificent tribute to the painstaking care and skill used in the engine's production.

WARNER AIRCRAFT CORPORATION
DETROIT, MICHIGAN

WARNER Scarab ENGINES

Arrival at Nome, Alaska April 23, 1929

The Takeoff for Siberia from the Snowfields at Nome

WESTERN UNION

Received at Corner Congress and Shelby Sts., Detroit, Mich.

NCG9 52 NL=NEWYORK NY 4   1929 MAY 5 AM 5 11

WARNER AIRCRAFT CO=
DETROIT MICH=

IN OVER TEN THOUSAND MILES FLYING FROM DETROIT TO NOME THEN SIBERIA AND RETURN TO NEWYORK SCARAB MOTOR FUNCTIONED PERFECTLY STOP MAINTENANCE FOR ENTIRE TRIP CONSISTED OF GREASING ROCKER ARMS AND OILING VALVE STEMS SIX TIMES ADJUSTING CLEARANCE ON TWO VALVES AND CLEANING ONE PLUG STOP THANKS FOR THE BUILT IN RELIABILITY=
         PARKER D CRAMER.

1929

A Moderately Priced Cabin Plane

For Business Executives — Salesmen
Transport Operators — Air Taxi Companies

$7200
Fly-away Wichita

The 4-place Cessna Monoplane, with the Warner Motor, is an ideal, moderately priced business airplane.

Dual control is provided, with the entire pilot's compartment finished in fabricoid. The passenger compartment is in green mohair. Baggage space for 4 suit-cases is conveniently placed just behind the passenger's seat.

Quantity production methods make possible the low price, as well as prompt deliveries.

CESSNA AIRCRAFT COMPANY
WICHITA, U.S.A.

"A Master's Expression"

Combining all the elements that make for the ultimate in air transportation—

Performance - Safety - Economy
Comfort - Convenience - Appearance

CESSNA AIRCRAFT COMPANY
WICHITA
U.S.A.

A RECORD to SHOOT AT

A Warner Scarab equipped Cessna flying from Wichita, Kansas, to Curtiss Field, Long Island, traveled a total of 1325 miles in 11 hours and 50 minutes (making one stop at St. Louis); on 64 gallons of gasoline.

This is an average of 112 miles per hour and better than 21 miles per gallon of gas.

In both air races and in regular commercial work the Warner Scarab is establishing remarkable records for reliability and economy.

> **MONOPLANES CESSNA**
> THE CESSNA AIRCRAFT COMPANY
> WICHITA
>
> OFFICE OF THE PRESIDENT
>
> April 6, 1929
>
> The Warner Aircraft Corp.
> Detroit, Michigan
>
> Gentlemen:
>
> We feel that you would be interested to know that in making deliveries to the Curtiss Flying Service that our Four Place Warner Powered Cabin Monoplane has been averaging twenty-one to twenty-three miles per gallon using Standard Aviation gasoline. We believe this a record for others to shoot at.
>
> CVC*G
>
> Yours very truly,

ECONOMY

Only 1-2/3 Cents per Mile

WARNER "Scarab" ENGINES
WARNER AIRCRAFT CORP.—DETROIT, MICH.

ECONOMY IN TRANSPORTATION GEARED FOR THIS SWIFT AGE LIES IN THE VALUE OF time saved AS WELL AS IN COST PER MILE OF TRAVEL

MONOPLANES CESSNA

Wichita to Alaska and Return
—13085 Miles in 127 Hours.

Parker Cramer flew a Monoplane Cessna over half way around the world in five days. His only maintenance was one spark plug cleaned and one valve clearance adjusted.

Monoplanes Cessna are being delivered to New York regularly for eastern buyers. They fly the 1325 miles in 11 to 12 hours. The fastest train time is over 40 hours.

Our records for three average trips to New York show a total cost for gas and oil per hour of $2.50, $2.36 and $1.76. Total cost of trips less than $25.00 each—slightly under 2c per mile. Train fare without Pullman for this trip is $55.54.

MONOPLANES CESSNA are not only the greatest time savers for the busy executive—but actual records prove that travel in these four-place cabin planes is also the most economical from a cost per mile standpoint.

Write our sales representatives for illustrated literature.

CESSNA
"A MASTER'S EXPRESSION"

Manufactured by The Cessna Aircraft Co., Wichita, U.S.A.

CURTISS FLYING SERVICE, INC.
Sole Sales Agents for United States and Canada
NEW YORK OFFICE, GARDEN CITY, LONG ISLAND

GLIDER PILOTS
WILL BE FUTURE TRANSPORT PILOTS

THE Cessna Aircraft Company -- aircraft pioneers -- forecast the present network of aerial transportation facilities; foresaw the demand for worthy airplanes -- and constructed the famous Monoplane Cessna.

Now these pioneers foresee the need for proper pilot training. In their effort towards meeting this need and training men economically and safely they have constructed with the same certainty of engineering principles embodied in Monoplanes Cessnas, the Monoplane Cessna Glider.

Crated, ready for shipment, $398 F. O. B. Wichita. Place your order now.

Attractive Dealer Proposition Awaits You.

CESSNA AIRCRAFT CO.
WICHITA, KANSAS

1930

Again WARNER comes thru!

Captures first place for Great Lakes Trophy on National Reliability Tour

Adding still further to the luster of Warner Achievements, Eddie Schneider, the young 18-year-old pilot, has just romped home with the Great Lakes Trophy awarded to the pilot in the National Reliability Tour, making the highest score with an engine less than 510 cubic inches.

Using a Cessna Monoplane now over a year old, powered with Warner engine No. 361, produced in August, 1929—the same plane and engine with which he broke the three Junior Transcontinental Records— Schneider entered the Reliability Tour without special preparation of any kind. No stream-lining of the plane—nor an engine overhaul.

Scoring 47,488 points, he was 11% in advance of his nearest competitor, who scored but 42,742.9. At the same time Schneider carried a 40% greater load—at a greater speed—with less rated horsepower.

Could any other test more conclusively demonstrate Warner Superiority?

WARNER AIRCRAFT CORPORATION
DETROIT,   MICHIGAN

WARNER "Scarab" ENGINES

CESSNA C34

Certified Performance

We are, quite naturally, proud of these trophies won at the 1935 National Air Races; and we are proud to have Cessna officially designated the World's Most Efficient Airplane—but actual day-in, day-out performance of the C34 is more important than trophies and titles to the private owner. That is the reason people are buying Cessnas as fast as we can build them.

Cessna C34, a four place cabin land monoplane, is powered with a Warner Super Scarab 145 h.p. engine. It has a cruising radius of over 500 miles, and flys 16 miles per gallon of fuel.

GUARANTEED PERFORMANCE—with wood prop:

High speed, fully loaded, sea level	162 m.p.h.
Cruising speed, fully loaded, sea level	143 m.p.h.
Landing speed, with wing flaps down	47 m.p.h.
Climb first minute	1,000 ft.
Service Ceiling	18,900 ft.

PRICE $4,985, f.a.f.

CESSNA AIRCRAFT CO.
Wichita, Kansas

THE NEW CESSNA C-37

FASTER The New C-37 Warner Powered Cessna is definitely faster. This New Cessna has been redesigned to give it still greater efficiency and performance.

BIGGER CABIN A much larger cabin, with roomy seats, lots of leg room and finer upholstery, adds a final touch of luxury to the "World's Most Efficient Airplane."

EASIER TO FLY The New C-37 Cessna with its ball bearing controls features greater maneuverability and ease of flying.

NEW EQUIPMENT Self operating, electrically powered wing flaps; electric gasoline gauge and ammeter; wind driven generator (in wing)—these are just a few of the features added to this new and finer Cessna monoplane.

WON BY CESSNA 3 CONSECUTIVE TIMES

—takes a good all around airplane to win the Detroit News Efficiency Trophy, *once*.

—takes an exceptionally efficient airplane to win it *twice* in succession!

—but only Cessna, the "World's Most Efficient Airplane," has won it *three consecutive times!*

CESSNA AIRCRAFT COMPANY
WICHITA, KANSAS, U.S.A.

We wouldn't have thought it possible to Improve the world's most Efficient Airplane, but—

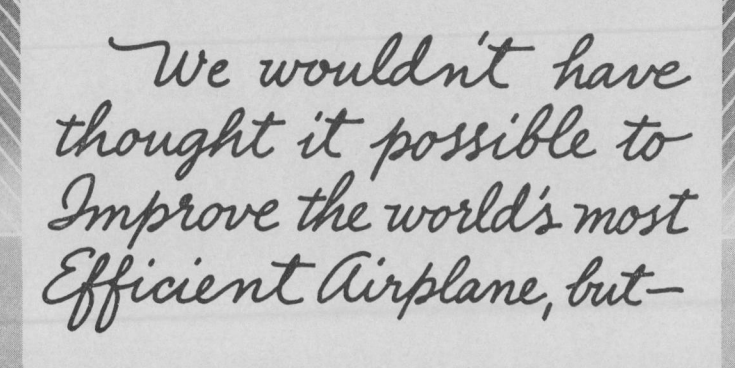

Cessna engineers are never satisfied!

Feature by feature . . . part by part . . . from nose to tail . . . former models of the World's Most Efficient Airplane were inspected, tested, analyzed and proved.

Advancements in design; improvements in materials; additional factors of stability and safety, and the new comforts and conveniences — long past the "laboratory stage," were included in

Cessna's New A-I-R-M-A-S-T-E-R

Among the achievements of Cessna engineers the **Airmaster** includes these: Larger useful load; more passenger and baggage space; increased stability in the air; new ground maneuverability; Cessna glide-control flap; cleaner lines; redesigned tail assembly; a new engine mounting that assures **security without** vibration, and many other features that put the Airmaster **'way ahead!**

See it! Fly it!
Let us arrange a demonstration.

CESSNA AIRCRAFT COMPANY
WICHITA, KANSAS, U.S.A.

EXPORT AGENT . AVIATION EQUIPMENT & EXPORT, INC. ★ CABLE ADDRESS "AVIQUIPO" ★ 25 BEAVER ST., NEW YORK, N.Y.

1938

Cessna "Airmaster" for 1938

● Cessna Aircraft Corp. is making its bid for the 1938 four-place cabin aircraft market with the *Airmaster*, an improved but basically similar version of the C-37.

Showing engineering refinements from nose to stern, the new airplane is noticeably different from its predecessor in the design of its landing gear. This undercarriage now provides 10.5" more tread than before without sacrificing the limiting strut angle, the added spread being obtained by substituting a one-piece, formed and heat-treated sponson tube for the built-up welded design previously used. The 3" × 5/32" chrome molybdenum 4130 tube used is first formed, the short joining tubes welded to it, and the unit then is heat-treated. Use of the joining tubes and wet asbestos packing prevents loss of heat-treatment qualities when the sponson is assembled into the fuselage.

A tapered metering pin used on the oleo of the new gear provides a variable rate of oil flow and consequent compensated shock absorption action. Full spring action for the 6" oleo travel insures a fully extended strut on every landing. Landing gear equipment also includes streamlined strut fairings, Warner 6.50 × 10 wheels, and mechanical brakes which may be operated from either of the front seats.

Fuselage structure is of chrome molybdenum steel tubing, covering being fabric aft, and aluminum alloy forward, the whole being protected against corrosion resulting from using the craft as a seaplane. U-type hangers attach the fuselage to the rear wing spar, and bushings through the forward spar permit the longerons to extend continuously from fore to aft. Fittings for the attachment of floats are provided. A noticeable change in the cabin is evident in the position of the front cross tube member which has been moved forward to a position behind the instrument panel. The pressed panel installed accommodates, as standard equipment, a Kollsman tachometer, altimeter, airspeed indicator, compass, oil pressure and temperature gauges. Space has been blanked out for any special instrument the purchaser may desire, and, in addition, the panel is arranged to take a number of extra instruments.

Placement of control stick sockets 6" forward provides greater ease of movement about the front seats which have been fitted with moulded rubber cushions. This not only provides comfort for the occupants, but also saves upholstery weight. Upholstery covering throughout is in broadcloth. Dual controls are standard equipment.

Wings are cantilevered, of the one-piece, tapered type. Spars are of laminated spruce, and the leading edge of the wing and tips is plywood covered. Another innovation in the *Airmaster* is the substitution of a belly flap for the previously used trailing edge type flap. The new flap has proven an effective means of controlling the glide and needs little trim to counteract its action.

The tail section is also a full cantilever type having a spruce fin and stabilizer, and chrome molybdenum steel tubing elevators and rudder. Rudder and fin have been redesigned over the previous model and the stern of the fuselage furthest aft has been made a fixed part of the fuselage instead of being incorporated with the rudder as in the past. Controls at principal points throughout are mounted on Fafnir ball bearings, giving smooth and frictionless action. Automatic locking type Arens push-pull units are used to prevent creeping of engine controls.

Ground handling has been aided by the use of a new tail wheel lock consisting of a spring-mounted pin which holds the tail wheel in the fore and aft position until the pilot disengages the pin for taxiing, at which time the unit becomes full swiveling through 360°.

Power is supplied by the 145 hp Series 50 Warner *Super Scarab* engine which is mounted on a newly-developed engine mount equipped with Lord rubber bushings, and made detachable at the one-piece stainless steel firewall. Tankage is provided for 35 gals. of fuel in the standard arrangement, but alternate provisions have been made to carry 45 or 52.5 gals.

Gross weight has been increased 100 lbs. over the previous model to 2350 lbs., with useful load now being 1000 lbs., an increase of 65 lbs. A total of 98 lbs. is provided for optional equipment installation.

Standard equipment, in addition to that already mentioned, includes a wing-mounted Hodge wind-driven generator, Eclipse direct drive starter, battery, radio bonding, Grimes navigation lights, and an ammeter and electric fuel gauge.

Specifications and estimated performances follow:

Wing span............34 feet 2 inches
Overall length..........24 feet 8 inches
Overall height....................7 feet
Wing area..............181 square feet
Empty weight..............1350 pounds
Payload ....574 pounds
Useful load................1000 pounds
Gross weight..............2350 pounds
Wing loading ....13 lbs./sq. ft.
Power loading............16.2 lbs./hp
Maximum speed......162 miles per hour
Cruising speed........143 miles per hour
Landing speed.........49 miles per hour
Rate of climb ....1000 feet/min.
Service ceiling.............18,000 feet
Cruising range...........525-785 miles

Outlines and side view of the 145 hp Warner-powered Cessna "Airmaster"

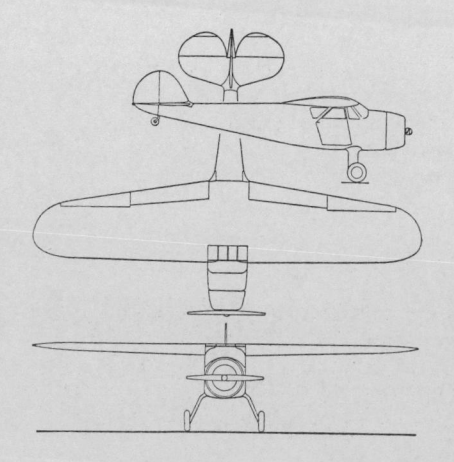

SMOOTH SAILING

★ THE CESSNA full cantilever monoplane has become known and is officially designated as the World's Most Efficient Airplane.

Even when the going is rough, Cessna's inherent stability levels out the bumps and turns in a performance of remarkable smoothness.

Cessna is the only airplane designed for private owners that offers the many advantages of full cantilever construction — there are no exposed wires or struts — from any angle Cessna is clean; efficient; smooth.

The Cessna Airmaster will carry an unusually large useful load at a smooth, unhurried cruising speed of more than 150 m.p.h. It has a convenient landing speed of less than 50 m.p.h.

Another thing that has made Cessna a favorite with pilots and owners in all parts of the world, particularly where fuel costs are high, is its exceptionally low gasoline consumption — more than 15 miles per gallon at cruising speed.

We'd like to have you find out about the Cessna — first hand.

CESSNA AIRCRAFT COMPANY WICHITA, KANSAS, U. S. A.

Export Agent — Aviation Equipment & Export, Inc.   ★   *Cable Address* — "Aviquipo" 25 Beaver Street, New York, N. Y.

1939

POINTS OF *Extra Value* IN THE
Cessna Airmaster

"The World's Most Efficient Airplane"

1. **Choice of Motors; either 145 (151 m. p. h. cruising) or 165 HP (157 m. p. h. cruising) Warner Super Scarab Engine.**
2. Hydraulic Brakes; with individual heel pedals and parking lever.
3. *Cantilever* Landing Gear; aerodynamically clean; sturdy.
4. Full Four-way Vision; you can see in air or on ground.
5. Roomy Cabin; wide door, ample passenger space, large baggage compartment.
6. Full *Cantilever* Wing Construction; no external struts or wires.
7. Electrically Actuated Wing Flaps; positive open, close and lock; Irreversible; Synchronized.
8. Superfine Finish; hand rubbed.
9. Full *Cantilever* Tail Group; complete streamlining spinner to stinger.
10. Full Swivel Tail Wheel with Positive Lock; extreme ground maneuverability.
11. Knife-edged Wing Tips, plywood covered; designed for speed and stability.
12. Efficiency; "World's Most Efficient Airplane," permanent title awarded in open competition.

Cessna owners are proud owners because they know Cessna excels in Beauty, Performance, and Economy.

CESSNA
AIRCRAFT COMPANY
WICHITA, KANSAS, U. S. A.

Export Agents . . . AVIATION EQUIPMENT & EXPORT, INC.
25 BEAVER ST., NEW YORK, N.Y. *Cable Address:* "AVIQUIPO"

1939

Fifth Avenue Styling

Home Town Economy

— and, if we may, *Big-Time Performance*, too!

The 1939 Cessna Airmaster gives *everything* you could desire and *much more* than you would expect in an airplane of this low price.

It brings you the trim, clean, ultra-streamlining made possible only through full cantilever design .. spacious comfort .. luxurious appointment .. extreme economy in fuel consumption and maintenance .. an airplane so beautiful that it makes you stop short, look long.

You'll own with pride .. and you'll fly with pleasure!

"THE WORLD'S MOST EFFICIENT AIRPLANE"

Cessna Aircraft Company

WICHITA, KANSAS, U. S. A.

Is it true what they say about CESSNA?

That Cessna is the "World's Most Efficient Airplane"?

That Cessna will really <u>cruise</u> at 143 m. p. h.?

That Cessna's landing speed is only 49 m. p. h.?

That Cessna will make about as many miles to a gallon of gasoline as any automobile?

That Cessna service ceiling is 18,000 feet?

That Cessna is easy to handle both in the air and on the ground?

That Cessna is convenient and comfortable for four large people?

That Cessna embodies <u>all</u> essential points of advanced aircraft design?

That Cessna is a safe plane—even for a novice?

Damn tootin' it's true!

CESSNA AIRCRAFT COMPANY
WICHITA, KANSAS . U. S. A.

Export Agent—Aviation Equipment & Export, Inc.
Cable Address . "AVIQUIPO" 25 Beaver St., New York, N.Y.

1939

CESSNA AIRMASTER FOR 1939

● The Cessna *Airmaster* for 1939 incorporates refinements in design and appearance intended to improve performance and enhance passenger comfort.

Construction basically is similar to the previous model in that the fuselage structure is of corrosion-proofed chrome molybdenum steel tubing covered forward with aluminum alloy, and aft of the landing gear point with fabric. Fairings are fastened by steel lugs. The cabin provides accommodations for four persons seated in twin tandem seats, the front seats facing dual controls and conveniently-located control columns. Visibility is enhanced by a moulded Plexiglas windshield unobstructed by structural members, and by curved side windows. Laidlaw upholstery and moulded rubber cushions improve appearance, and comfort is further aided by the availability of four ventilators. Instruments are mounted on an indirectly lighted panel having space for additional instruments other than the following which are provided as standard equipment: Kollsman tachometer, altimeter, airspeed indicator, compass, oil pressure and oil temperature gauges; ammeter.

The characteristic Cessna cantilever wing consists of two laminated spruce spars, rigidly braced in torsion by deep drag trusses and double drag wire bracing. Covering of the leading edge and tips is plywood, and of the balance of the wing, fabric. Basic airfoil section is the NACA 2412 series, the wing tapering in thickness and planform throughout the span.

Ailerons are hinged on self-aligning Fafnir bearings and are statically and dynamically balanced. An aluminum alloy split type flap is located between the aileron and fuselage just forward of the rear spar. Actuated electrically, the flap stops automatically in the fully extended position. It can also be lowered to any increment of the full down position by the pilot who is provided with a switch for this purpose in the cockpit at the left of the instrument panel within convenient reach.

Power is supplied by a 145 hp Warner *Super Scarab* engine equipped with a Curtiss fixed pitch propeller, and mounted on a detachable engine mount suspended at the one-piece stainless steel firewall with Lord rubber bushings. Tankage is provided for 35 gals. of fuel in the standard arrangement, but provision has been made for carrying either 45 gals. or 52.5 gals. An electrically operated fuel gauge is provided.

Additional standard equipment includes: a wing-mounted wind-driven Hodge generator, Eclipse direct drive starter, battery, Grimes navigation lights.

Instrument panel, large entrance door, sliding seat and interior details of the Airmaster

The Sportsman Test Pilot

James B. Taylor, Jr., Flies the Warner 165-powered Cessna

I HAVE been anxious for some time to fly the latest Cessna powered by the Warner 165 horsepower engine, and recently was able to do so through the courtesy of Larry Faunce, of the Warner Aircraft Corporation, who had flown the company ship to Roosevelt Field.

There is little, if any, difference between the 165 and the 145 horsepower Cessna models for 1940 and last year's models. The chief differences are a slightly wider undercarriage, the location of the flaps at about the middle of the under side of the wing instead of on the bottom of the fuselage, and a considerably improved interior.

The outward appearance of the little Cessna is excellent. It has very clean lines that assure a high speed. Cessna is the only manufacturer making an unbraced wing which is covered entirely with fabric instead of plywood or metal. The company has pioneered this for many years. While there was some trouble with high powered models in the very early days of Cessna, due largely to lack of balance on the ailerons, no trouble has occurred from it since then.

The method of entering the cabin is a little difficult until one gets used to it. A sort of routine is followed. The pilot gets in first, followed by the occupant of the other front seat. This right front seat, by the way, slides back against the rear seat to facilitate reaching the two front places. When it is in the forward position, the passengers may enter. Once seated, I was agreeably surprised at the amount of room. It is true that the front spar is fairly close to the back of one's head and I imagine a long-legged pilot, with the seat way back, might be cramped. However, I was very comfortable and vision was excellent.

The instrument panel is nicely laid out. The Warner company's ship has a few extras, such as thermocouples, etc. However, there was plenty of room for extra instruments. This particular ship is equipped with one-way radio—a small Lear receiver. It also has a starter, generator and a Curtiss-Reed metal propeller, which apparently gives considerably better performance on this ship, although the wooden prop is the type that is fitted as standard.

When the time came to fly this ship I unfortunately was unable to include any passengers, so only had the opportunity of flying it solo. However, it is a matter of record that the ship carries four people and considerable baggage and that its performance is still outstanding.

The undercarriage and taxying seemed to be very smooth and comfortable. The brakes were adequate. A tailwheel lock is fitted for landing or taxying in a strong wind. The tanks were filled when I flew it and the take-off was excellent, the climb being steep and rapid. The controls on this little ship, as is the case with most Cessnas, are rather heavy. This is more mechanical than anything else, as they are heavy on the ground at rest.

However, the ship is so sensitive that this is not particularly noticeable, except that both hands are required on the stick in a vertical bank because the ailerons are heavy at any speed. The ship is very stable and can be flown hands off indefinitely. Good turns can be made without use of the rudder, and fair turns can be made using only the rudder. The stall is very gentle. In fact, it was very difficult to stall it at all if pulled up slowly with power on or off in the light condition. Undoubtedly, it would stall a little faster with full load. However, there was no tendency for a wing to drop viciously.

The ventilation was excellent and the heat seemed to be adequate. Heat was not necessary the day I was flying, but when turned on, plenty of heat was available. The ship was reasonably quiet and the vision in the air from the pilot's standpoint was excellent.

I was particularly interested in the flaps because, as anyone who has consistently read these articles knows, I seem to have objected either to the lack of flaps or to their being inadequate on most of the ships I have flown. I was much pleased with the Cessna flaps, which are electrically operated by a switch conveniently placed in the center of the instrument panel. They give practically 100 per cent drag and very little increase in lift, which, after all, is all that is necessary in a reasonably lightly loaded aircraft. There was practically no change of trim on putting them down. If anything, the ship seemed to get slightly tail heavy.

Stall characteristics, power on and power off, with flaps down were just as gentle as with them up. Putting the flaps up, either in a glide or in flight caused no sinking sensation. The ship merely picked up speed. Yet they caused the ship to come in in quite a steep glide with plenty of vision forward.

I was also agreeably surprised at the fact that the rudder, even in a fairly slow glide, was adequate for gentle forward sideslips, which is not the case in many airplanes. In all maneuvers with the flaps down, including stalls, no burble, or buffeting, was noticeable on the tail. Coming into the field, even with excessive speed, the flaps cut down any tendency to float.

However, on landing it was almost necessary to use both hands on the stick in order to get the tail down. Then it was possible to get the tail on the ground a second or so before the main wheel and make a very nice short landing. The undercarriage again seemed excellent and I imagine the ship could stand a considerable amount of mishandling without any serious consequences.

With regard to top speed, there is no question but that the ship is fast. However, it is doubtful if it is much faster than the 145 horsepower job. The main gain from the extra horsepower is in the climb, which is very useful for getting in and out of small fields, particularly in view of the fact that the added gas consumption is negligible. Mr. Faunce assured me that in flying all over the country he had averaged about 150 miles per hour cruising which is really very adequate for 165 horsepower.

In conclusion, I would say that the Cessna is undoubtedly the most *efficient* airplane for its horsepower and size in the country. Its flying qualities are excellent and while one would dislike to ride for eight or ten hours at a stretch in the rear seat, it is adequately comfortable. For two people on long trips, it provides a great deal of space and capacity for baggage. The only criticism I have of it is that I think the control forces could be lightened considerably which would then make it a much more pleasant airplane to fly.

TWIN TWIN IN EVERYTHING BUT PRICE!

Cessna T50 Twin

The CESSNA T50 TWIN has met with a gratifying acceptance during the past year. Deliveries to both the Civil Aeronautics Authority and commercial purchasers are proceeding rapidly on schedule. Demand has necessitated an extensive enlargement of the CESSNA factory.

The popularity of the five-place T50 TWIN is due to its exceptional construction features and performance characteristics plus the fact that this outstanding twin-engined airplane is offered within the price range of single-engined planes of comparable performance and appointments.

Cruising 191 M.P.H., the surprisingly low-priced CESSNA T50 TWIN with its flawless flight characteristics, plus its many twin-engined advantages, is the airplane you have always wanted. Full details will gladly be sent to you upon request.

- Twin SAFETY
- Twin PERFORMANCE
- Twin COMFORT
- Twin PRESTIGE
- Twin BEAUTY
- Twin MANEUVERABILITY
- Twin STABILITY
- Twin LUXURY
- Twin QUIETNESS
- Twin SPEED

AND THE *Airmaster*

The single-engined CESSNA AIRMASTER is setting up new sales records, too. Long recognized as "The World's Most Efficient Airplane," because of its speed, economy, comfort and easy-flying characteristics, the AIRMASTER carries four people fifteen miles per gallon of fuel at 157 M.P.H., and is ideal for business or pleasure use. Your request will bring complete details and prices.

CESSNA AIRCRAFT COMPANY
WICHITA, KANSAS, U.S.A.

TECHNICAL DESCRIPTION

The Cessna T-50 twin engined trainer is ruggedly constructed so as to meet the severe usage of a training ship. Soundly engineered by the men who have designed the "World's Most Efficient Airplane," this new Cessna is built to the same high standards which have made Cessna airplanes well known throughout the entire world.

FUSELAGE

The fuselage of the Cessna T-50 is constructed of 4130X steel tubing and carefully strengthened for high localized loads. This type of construction was adopted due to its simplicity and unexcelled ease of repair. The fuselage is attached to the wing by four principal fittings, which fittings are integral parts of the structure.

WING

The full cantilever wing is continuous from tip to tip and is similar to other wings which have been built by Cessna over a period of many years.

The spruce spars are held rigid torsionally by heavy double type drag wire bracing. The strength of the wing is further enhanced by plywood covered tips and leading edge.

The motors are supported from the two spars by a steel tube nacelle structure which ties the spars rigidly together at this point.

The gasoline tanks are located within the wing just inboard of the nacelles, this section of the wing being covered by heavy plywood.

Trailing edge flaps are used. The flaps are actuated electrically through an irreversible screw mechanism. The ailerons are statically balanced Friese type.

FIXED TAIL SURFACES

The construction of the fixed tail surface is essentially the same as of the wing. Both the stabilizer and the fin have two spruce spars and are covered entirely by plywood which insures a maximum stiffness both in bending and in torsion.

MOVABLE TAIL SURFACES

Movable tail surfaces are constructed of 4130X steel tubing and sheet. They are hinged at the fixed surfaces by grease-sealed ball bearings.

CONTROL SYSTEM

The control system consists of extra flexible steel aircraft cable running over ball bearing pulleys. Where advantageous, push pull rods are used in lieu of cables.

LANDING GEAR

The landing gear consists of a cantilever shock absorber which is carried and supported in a heavy fork. When retracted the wheel rises almost vertically which keeps its position well ahead of the airplane's center of gravity at all times. The entire landing gear is mounted on ball bearings, the retraction being made possible through the use of a screw which is driven by an electric motor. This electric motor has a built-in clutch which automatically disengages in case of motor failure, thus enabling the pilot to retract the gear manually. The landing gear oleos are of the oil-air type and have a full 8-inch travel. Hydraulic braked wheels are provided.

The tail wheel is equipped with an automatic locking device which holds rigidly in fore and aft position during landing and take-off periods. It may be released at any time for full 360° swivel. An oil-spring oleo provides the shock absorbing.

CORROSION PROOFING

Care has been taken to protect the primary structure against corrosion. Protection is provided by zinc chromate primer and navy gray enamel.

28 YEARS OF CONTINUOUS PROGRESS

The first Cessna was flown April 14, 1911 — 28 years ago. Since that date, Cessna designers and engineers have steadily improved the aircraft built by Cessna. The Cessna Airmaster (single motored, Warner powered) was officially designated and given the permanent title of "The World's Most Efficient Airplane." Today Cessnas are built in this modern well-equipped factory which is manned by capable and experienced airplane builders.

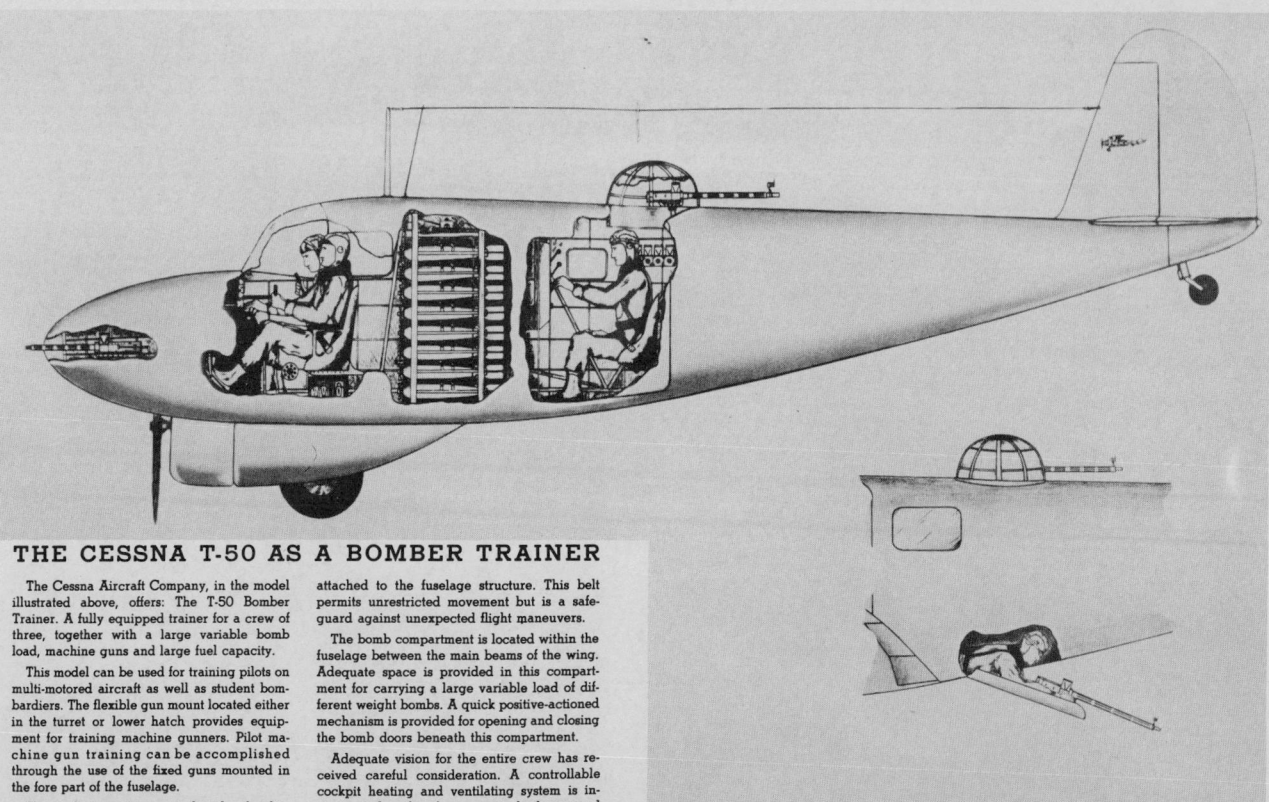

THE CESSNA T-50 AS A BOMBER TRAINER

The Cessna Aircraft Company, in the model illustrated above, offers: The T-50 Bomber Trainer. A fully equipped trainer for a crew of three, together with a large variable bomb load, machine guns and large fuel capacity.

This model can be used for training pilots on multi-motored aircraft as well as student bombardiers. The flexible gun mount located either in the turret or lower hatch provides equipment for training machine gunners. Pilot machine gun training can be accomplished through the use of the fixed guns mounted in the fore part of the fuselage.

The student gunner or student bombardier is provided with a flexible gun belt securely attached to the fuselage structure. This belt permits unrestricted movement but is a safeguard against unexpected flight maneuvers.

The bomb compartment is located within the fuselage between the main beams of the wing. Adequate space is provided in this compartment for carrying a large variable load of different weight bombs. A quick positive-actioned mechanism is provided for opening and closing the bomb doors beneath this compartment.

Adequate vision for the entire crew has received careful consideration. A controllable cockpit heating and ventilating system is incorporated so that the necessity for heavy and cumbersome flying equipment is eliminated.

1940

VIA AIR To Canada From Cessna

CESSNA AIRCRAFT COMPANY — WICHITA, KANSAS, U.S.A.
CONTRACTORS TO THE U.S. ARMY AND THE ROYAL CANADIAN AIR FORCE

1941

for the hard jobs – the **CESSNA T50 TWIN**

CESSNA AIRCRAFT COMPANY — WICHITA, KANSAS, U. S. A.
CONTRACTORS TO THE U. S. ARMY AND THE ROYAL CANADIAN AIR FORCE

for National Defense **CESSNA AT-8**

CESSNA AIRCRAFT COMPANY — **WICHITA, KANSAS, U. S. A.**
CONTRACTORS TO THE U. S. ARMY AND THE ROYAL CANADIAN AIR FORCE

bomber pilots?

In the United States...

THE Cessna Aircraft Company has delivered more twin-engined bomber-pilot trainers than all other U. S. aircraft manufacturers combined. For 1942 we pledge ourselves to continue and surpass our past record of consistently exceeding delivery schedules ... to do our full part in the all-out fight for Democracy.

CESSNA *Aircraft Company*

WICHITA, KANSAS, U.S.A.

CONTRACTORS TO THE U. S. ARMY AND THE ROYAL CANADIAN AIR FORCE

1942

Bradley Farm, Wichita, Kansas

new • more powerful
FOR 1948

Cessna 140

The lovely instrument panel is as functional as it is beautiful. And you have a choice between two eye-resting, two-tone finishes. The panel is shock mounted and indirectly lighted. Note, too, the wide rudder pedals and toe brakes.

Wide windows and one-piece windshield, without annoying braces, gives you exceptional visibility in the 140 and 120. And the airline-type ventilators give you complete control over the volume and direction of fresh air.

Cowling can be quickly stripped without removing the propeller — just one of the many maintenance saving features to cut operating costs on the Cessna 140 and 120.

Exceptionally easy riding — greatly increased safety — absolutely no maintenance — that is Cessna's patented safety landing gear. Installed on over 7,000 Cessnas, this gear has proved itself.

... take to the HIGH

There's a lot to be done these days. And there's just one way to get it all done . . by taking to the skyways. Thousands of users have already put their planes in t same category of necessity as their cars. For everyday use has shown them th can *literally stretch time* by taking to the highways of the sky.

Business trips that used to take most of a day can be made in a couple hours. Vacation spots become regular weekend places for fun and relaxatio Sales territories can be doubled and tripled . . . without increasing the time cost of coverage. And traveling is so much easier — so much more comfortab

For business and pleasure, look to the New Cessna for '48. Here's a n conception of comfort, fine appointments and outstanding performance.

The new 90-horsepower Continental engine offers greater performance shorter take-off, quicker climb, faster cruise. The lower rpm assures quietness.

The luxurious interior assures you of comfortable, enjoyable flying. Eas adjustable seats with no-sag springs, thickly padded with sponge rubber, give y restful comfort for the full 4½-hour cruising range of the speedy Cessna 1

The beauty of the two-toned instrument panel is as functional as it is e appealing. The readability of the instruments, the minimum of switches and c trols placed for easy use, the eye-resting color of the panel . . . all contribute your ease and comfort — to your pride in owning the finest aircraft in its cla

And, of course, all the little things have been thought of. Conveniently plac ash tray; cigarette lighter; directional, airline type air ventilators; handholds getting in and out of the cabin; fine all-wool upholstery with genuine leather t that makes for beauty and durability — nothing has been left undone. And co plete comfort is yours in the coldest weather with the exceptionally efficient hea available for the 140 and 120.

The famous Cessna patented safety landing gear is another outstand feature. In two years of service on over 7,000 airplanes, this chrome vanadi

TIME FLIES... S

ay..

...eel gear has proved its outstanding qualities of safety and tough reliability. You'll ...nd that it's the easiest riding you've ever taxied. It literally erases the bumps. ...ou'll find that it'll take the roughest shocks you can subject it to, that it combats ...round looping tendencies, that it makes cross-wind landings a cinch. And best of ...ll, it requires no maintenance — only a simple visual check at 100-hour inspections.

As to the flying characteristics . . . well, you'll have to fly the Cessna to really ...ppreciate them. But we can say you've pleasant experience coming. Short takeoff, ...uick climb, fast cruising . . . and yet, in spite of the Cessna's high performance, ...ou'll find a slow landing speed and stability at slow speeds that makes it one of ...he easiest and safest airplanes you've ever flown.

See the Cessna 140 today. Check all the features and compare. Fly it and ...ompare. From every standpoint, we know you'll find Cessna the finest.

(Wheel pants shown are extra equipment.)

Cessna 140

Quick-acting, full range flaps are a feature of the 140. These all-metal flaps give positive control of the glide angle from shallow to steep. They also permit unusually short take-offs from extremely short fields.

Licensed for 80 pounds, the Cessna baggage compartment gives you plenty of room for a man's two-suiter, a lady's fortnighter, and two brief cases or other small pieces of luggage . . . in addition to two people and full tanks of gas.

Versatility and utility of the Cessna can be greatly extended by the use of floats and skis. Approved by the CAA for both seaplane and skiplane operation, your flight horizons are unlimited by terrain. Flying to your favorite ski slopes or winter hunting grounds . . . flying to your favorite fishing lake can become as commonplace as it is easy. These are "must" items for the charter operator.

SHOULD YOU!

Cessna 120

ALL YOURS
on the Cessna 120 and 140

Basically, the 120 is the same airplane as the 140, but is priced much lower without starter, generator, flaps, and extra luxurious appointments. But you'll find the same good looks and quality construction. Upholstery of Redolite leather . . . a good-looking, tough, and washable material made by DuPont . . . covers seat cushions, seat back, and door panels. The floor is covered with long-wearing carpeting. A generous amount of soundproofing is used at the firewall. A two-toned, shock mounted instrument panel adds distinction to the handsome 120.

With a much lower initial investment, but with virtually the same performance, the 120 makes an ideal trainer and cross-country charter plane for the operator. Low cost of maintenance and operation, exceptional comfort, and low noise level offer additional advantages . . . not only to the operator but to the instructor, student and owner as well. A complete electrical system with starter, generator, battery, and lights may be added to the 120 when desired.

1948 SPECIFICATIONS

	Model 120	Model 140
ENGINE: CONTINENTAL	85 h.p.	90 h.p.
TOP SPEED	Over 120 m.p.h.	Over 125 m.p.h.
CRUISING SPEED	Over 100 m.p.h.	Over 105 m.p.h.
CRUISING RANGE	Over 4½ hrs.	4½ hrs.
RATE OF CLIMB (sea level)	680 ft. per min.	690 ft. per min.
SERVICE CEILING	15,500 ft.	15,600 ft.
LANDING SPEED	41 m.p.h.	41 m.p.h.
GROSS WEIGHT	1,450 lbs.	1,450 lbs.
EMPTY WEIGHT	785 lbs.	860 lbs.
FUEL CAPACITY	25 gals.	25 gals.
SPAN	32 ft. 10 in.	32 ft. 10 in.
LENGTH	21 ft. 6 in.	21 ft. 6 in.
HEIGHT	6 ft. 3¼ in.	6 ft. 3¼ in.
WING AREA (including fuselage)	159.3 sq. ft.	159.3 sq. ft.
WING LOADING (per sq. ft.)	9.1 lbs.	9.1 lbs.
POWER LOADING (per h.p.)	17.1 lbs.	16.1 lbs.

STANDARD EQUIPMENT

	Model 120	Model 140
ASH TRAY	x	x
AIRSPEED	x	x
ALTIMETER	x	x
AMMETER		x
BATTERY		x
CARBURETOR AIR FILTER	x	x
CARBURETOR HEATER	x	x
CABIN AIR VENTS	x	x
CIGARETTE LIGHTER		x
COMPASS	x	x
DUAL CONTROL WHEELS	x	x
ENGINE MUFFLERS	x	x
GAS GAUGES	x	x
GENERATOR		x
HYDRAULIC BRAKES	x	x
LANDING LIGHT WIRING AND BRACKETS		x
MAP COMPARTMENT		x
MIXTURE CONTROL		x
NAVIGATION LIGHTS		x
OIL PRESSURE	x	x
OIL TEMPERATURE	x	x
OVERHEAD WINDOWS		x
PARKING BRAKE		x
REAR WINDOWS (TWO)		x
RUBBER FOAM SEAT CUSHIONS	x	x
SHOCK MOUNTED INSTRUMENT PANEL	x	x
STARTER		x
STEERABLE TAIL WHEEL	x	x
TACHOMETER	x	x
WING FLAPS		x

Cessna 140
1951

Metal propeller, wheel pants, landing lights, pictured are optional equipment at extra cost

The New ALL M

Why should you own a Cessna?
Sure, it's fun, and easy to fly but
will it pay? Let's analyze
it as a tool to perform any
travel assignment,
business or pleasure.
Take a map and with your town
in the center, draw a circle with
110 mile radius and a
second circle twice as large, a
third circle, etc. Every town, farm
and landsite within the first
circle will be less than one
hour away in a Cessna 140.
Those within the next circle less
than two hours away, and so on.
How sharply will this cut your travel time?
With this tool, how much more could you
do, how much more could you earn?
Mr. A—— of Atlanta reports that he now
covers his territory twice where he used
to do it once — is at home 3 times as
much — and is earning more at less
traveling cost with his Cessna than
formerly with his automobile.
You'll find excellent downtown airports
in many cities, such as Chicago,
Detroit, Cleveland, Milwaukee, Oklahoma City,
and Kansas City, etc. Wherever you
go, your Cessna will take you close to your exact
destination — quickly, thriftily, pleasantly.
It's the right tool for your travel!
Considering the cold facts — can you
afford *not* to own this Cessna?
It's easy to fly and easy to learn to fly.

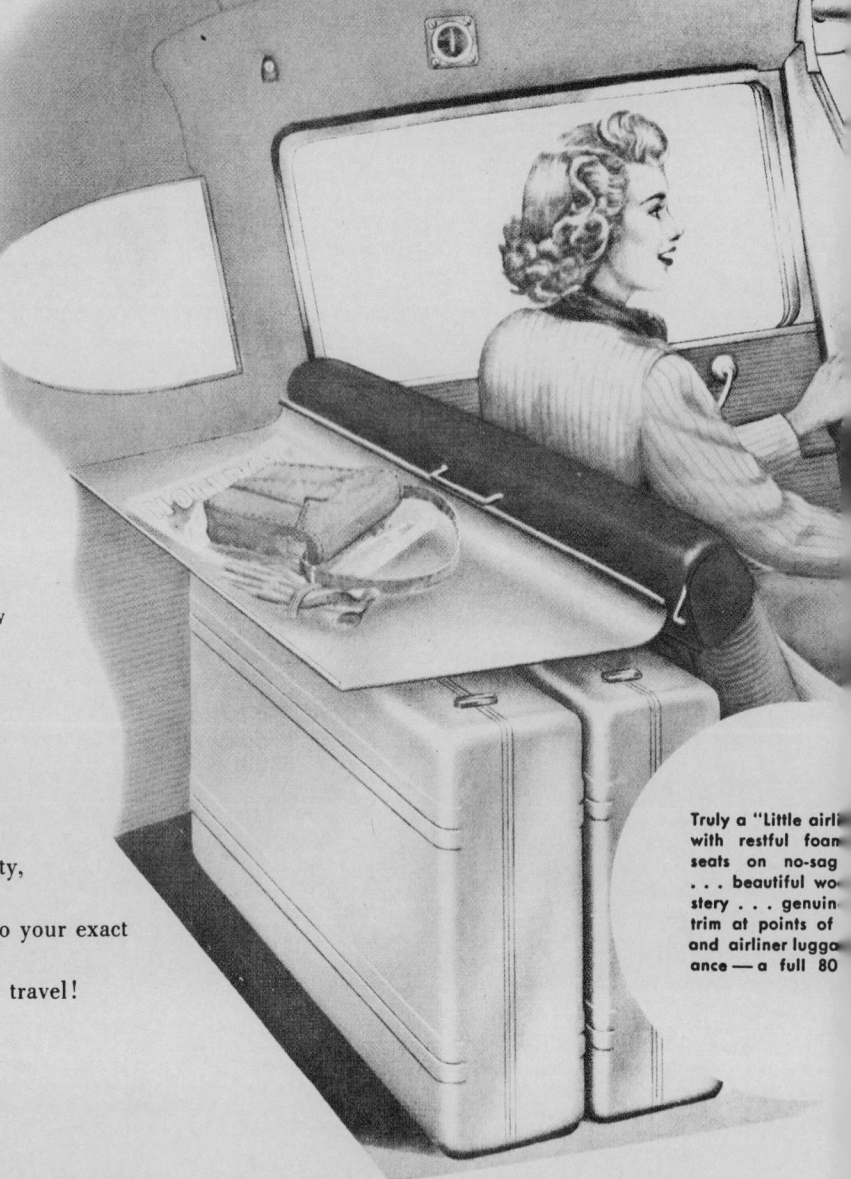

Truly a "Little airli
with restful foam
seats on no-sag
... beautiful wo
stery ... genuin
trim at points of
and airliner lugga
ance — a full 80

Patented safety landing gear, proved on some 10,000 Cessnas, provides taxiing ease, safety in cross-winds, zero upkeep cost*

Hydraulic toe brakes give you easy, positive stopping and turning control, for safe ground maneuvering and parking

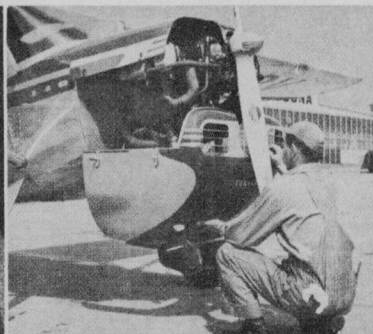

Cowling is quickly removable without disturbing propeller, giving easy access to the entire power plant and its accessories

New all-metal airliner type co high-efficiency all-metal, semi-ca strut ... quick-action all-metal fla able tail wheel ... shock-mounted

Cessna 140

You will be proud to own the new Cessna 140 — beautiful inside and outside, with outstanding flight characteristics. Take a good look at this all-metal 140 with the semi-cantilever tapered metal wing. Sure, it costs more to build the wing that way — but it makes a better airplane, cleaner aerodynamically, with superb aileron control. And you'll find this easy to fly Cessna 140 gives you a smoother, more pleasant ride than you thought possible in any airplane of its weight class.

Look at that landing gear — proved all over the world on some 10,000 Cessnas, large and small — an outstanding postwar design advancement. Ask any Cessna owner how it acts on rough fields, in cross-winds — whether he's spent any money maintaining it — what he honestly thinks of this unique Cessna major feature.

Open the door and enjoy the rich quality of the smartly styled interior. See how beauty and utility blend in the instrument panel styling. Check the handy map compartment that holds full size sectional maps, normally folded. Notice the unobstructed windshield vision — the ample, quiet, airliner-type controlled ventilation system. And this cabin stays snug and warm in the coldest weather. Relax on thick foam rubber seats over no-sag springs, and seat backs that adjust for your complete comfort. Enjoy the quiet that comes from Cessna's ample spun glass insulation and efficient, stainless steel engine mufflers.

Look at the new Cessna 140 with an eye to maintenance. It's all metal. Ball or roller bearings at all major wearing points. No landing gear upkeep — and a minimum of maintenance on that good Continental engine, or anywhere on the airplane. The honest quality designed and built into this fine new Cessna 140 will show up as it gives you thousands upon thousands of miles of reliable, pleasant, trouble-free travel. Some of the many special features in the superb Cessna 140 are explained in the pictures below.

*See page 4 for Standard Equipment

op to bottom . . . new, low drag, single wing l . . . full-swivelling, steer- are typical "140" features

Enjoy fresh air where and when you want it, inside your 140's quiet, soundproofed cabin, from adjustable airline-type ventilators

Full airline luggage allowance is yours, with 80 lbs. licensed capacity and ample space for two large bags and more

For family trips, you can fit this safe, comfortable "tot seat" into the usual luggage area, and take the children along on tour

Cessna 140

THE Cessna 140 MEANS BUSINESS

...MORE CONTACTS, MORE BUSINESS FOR YOU!

STANDARD EQUIPMENT
Either 85 h.p. or 90 h.p.

- Ash Tray
- Airspeed
- Altimeter
- Ammeter
- Battery (12-volt)
- Carburetor Air Filter
- Carburetor Heater
- Cabin Air Vents
- Cigarette Lighter
- Compass
- Dual Control Wheels and Rudder Pedals
- Engine Mufflers
- Flaps, full adjustable, 43-degree travel
- Gas Gauges
- Generator
- Hydraulic Brakes — Toe Operated
- Instrument Lighting, Indirect, Rheostat Controlled
- Landing Light Wiring and Brackets
- Map Compartment
- Mixture Control
- Navigation Lights
- Oil Pressure Gauge
- Oil Temperature Gauge
- Overhead Windows
- Parking Brake
- Rear Windows (Two)
- Rubber Foam Seat Cushions — No-Sag Spring Construction
- Shock-Mounted Instrument Panel
- Stall Warning Indicator
- Starter
- Steerable, Full-Swiveling Tail Wheel
- Tachometer
- Tie Down Rings
- Wood Propeller

MODEL 140
1949 Specifications
With McCauley Propeller*

	90 h.p.	85 h.p.
Engine: Continental	90 h.p.	85 h.p.
Top Speed	Over 125 m.p.h.	Over 120 m.p.h.
Cruising Speed	Over 110 m.p.h.	Over 105 m.p.h.
Cruising Range	4½ hrs.	Over 4½ hrs.
Rate of Climb (sea level)	690 ft. per min.	680 ft. per min.
Service Ceiling	15,600 ft.	15,500 ft.
Landing Speed	41 m.p.h.	41 m.p.h.
Gross Weight	1,500 lbs.	1,500 lbs.
Empty Weight	900 lbs.	900 lbs.
Fuel Capacity	25 gals.	25 gals.
Span	33 ft. 4 in.	33 ft. 4 in.
Length	21 ft. 6 in.	21 ft. 6 in.
Height	6 ft. 3¾ in.	6 ft. 3¾ in.
Wing Area (inc. fuselage)	159.6 sq. ft.	159.6 sq. ft.
Wing Loading (per sq. ft.)	9.75 lbs.	9.75 lbs.
Power Loading (per h.p.)	16.7 lbs.	17.6 lbs.

CESSNA AIRCRAFT COMPANY
WICHITA, KANSAS, U. S. A.

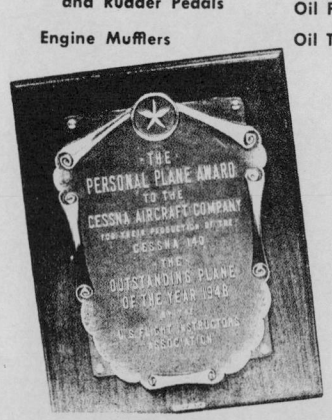

AIRCRAFT AND ACCESSORIES PRICE LIST
1962 CESSNA MODEL 150

Effective September 18, 1961

STANDARD	F.A.F. Wichita, Kansas	$7,495.00
TRAINER	F.A.F. Wichita, Kansas	$8,400.00
"INTER-CITY" COMMUTER	F.A.F. Wichita, Kansas	$8,995.00
CESSNA NAV-O-MATIC	Installed Weight 9.5 pounds	$995.00

EASY TO HANDLE...
EASIER TO LAND
AND TAKE OFF...
EASIEST TO FLY!

Why? In the 150 you have "Land-O-Matic" gear! Truly Cessna — long famous, maintenance free and proven as the industry's finest. Check over the wide tread and long wheelbase. Here is a landing gear at its best... ideal for unfaltering, arrow-straight landings, and the smoothest taxiing and ground handling qualities you could ask for. Chrome vanadium steel leaf spring struts cheerfully forgive the errors of student pilots and cushion landings on the bumpiest sod. The nose wheel quenches shocks through an air-oil oleo strut. A built-in dampener steadies the nose gear. The nose wheel is steered by the rudder pedals 10° from center to right or left. Then, for sharp turns, it swivels freely 20° more on either side. Upon takeoff, it automatically locks on center to assure straight-ahead "fly-in" landings.

Service proved hydraulic brakes, toe operated by pedals on the rudder controls, provide fast, safe stops and superior ground maneuverability. The cool running, long-life, four-ply nylon tubeless tires are interchangeable on all wheels. Optional speed fairings add the finishing touch of high style and aerodynamic efficiency.

★ ★ ★ ★ ★

CERTIFIED CESSNA-CLEAN...
A GUARANTEE OF
AERODYNAMIC EXCELLENCE

Step back to the tail and see how the 150 measures up to this guarantee. You'll find it is every inch a Cessna. The horizontal stabilizer is a full ten feet wide — with cantilever design — assuring swift control response to engine power. Its leading edge is aerodynamically clean, unquestionably strong. A

Step Beyond the Ordinary

An extra dimension of fun, pleasure To something special. A sense of freedom in performing and pride. aerobatic maneuvers.

Barrel Rolls • Aileron Rolls • Single Snaps • Loops • Immelmans • Cuban 8's • Spins • Vertical Reversements

Colorful stripes and checkerboard accents identify the Aerobat as a special breed. Aerobatics encourage the highest standards of discipline and in the process help pilots become the best they can be. It builds their confidence and helps them acquire the finesse and precise airspeed management skills demanded by aerobatic flying. The 150 Aerobat is particularly appropriate for aerobatic flight instruction and for the continuing self-development of the dedicated pilot.

The Aerobat reinvents flying fun. It welcomes you to master the art of aerobatics with only a few hours of proper instruction.

Genealogy of Aircraft

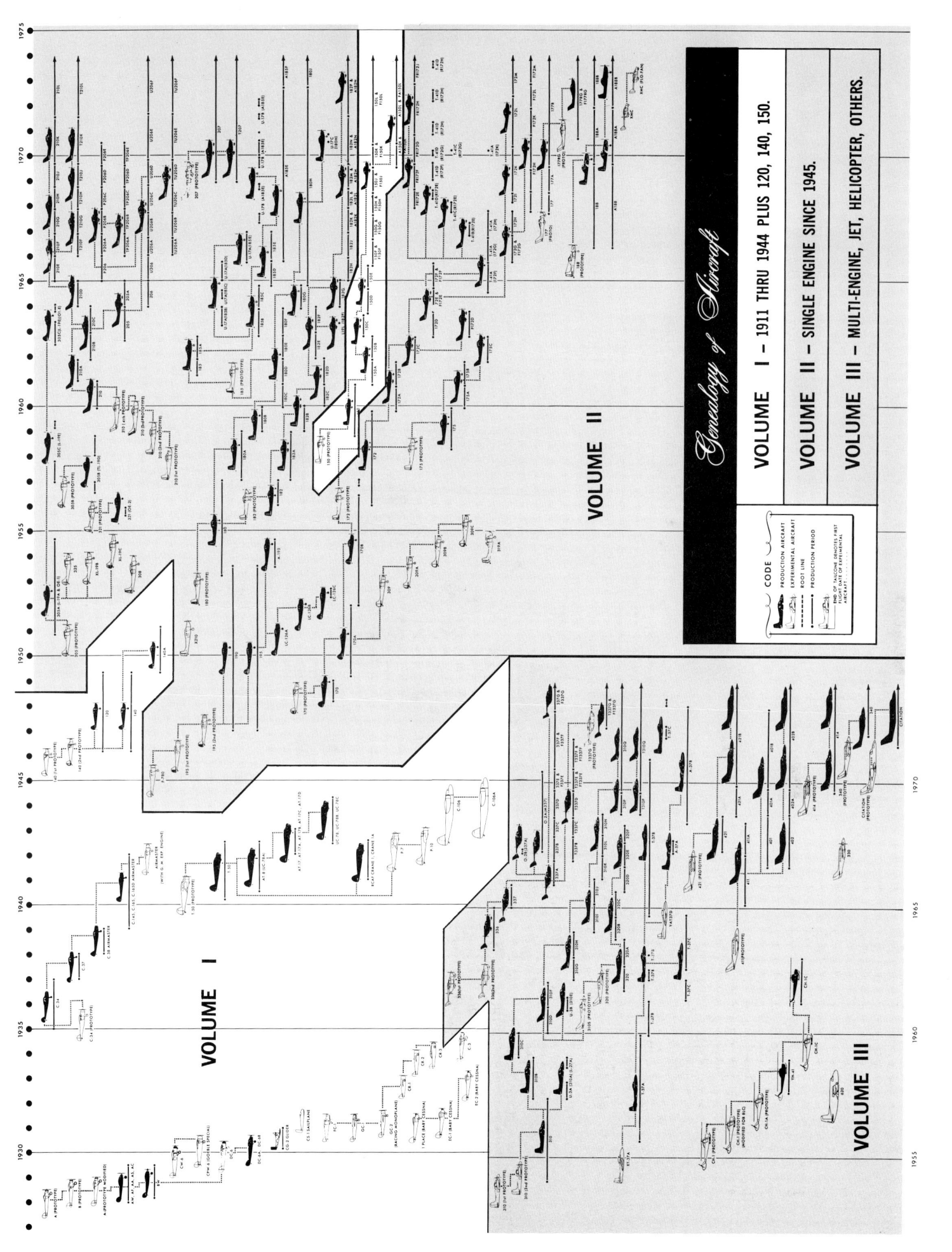

VOLUME I — 1911 THRU 1944 PLUS 120, 140, 150.

VOLUME II — SINGLE ENGINE SINCE 1945.

VOLUME III — MULTI-ENGINE, JET, HELICOPTER, OTHERS.

CODE:
- PRODUCTION AIRCRAFT
- EXPERIMENTAL AIRCRAFT
- ROOT LINE
- PRODUCTION PERIOD
- END OF TAILCONE DENOTES FIRST FLIGHT DATE OF EXPERIMENTAL AIRCRAFT.

93

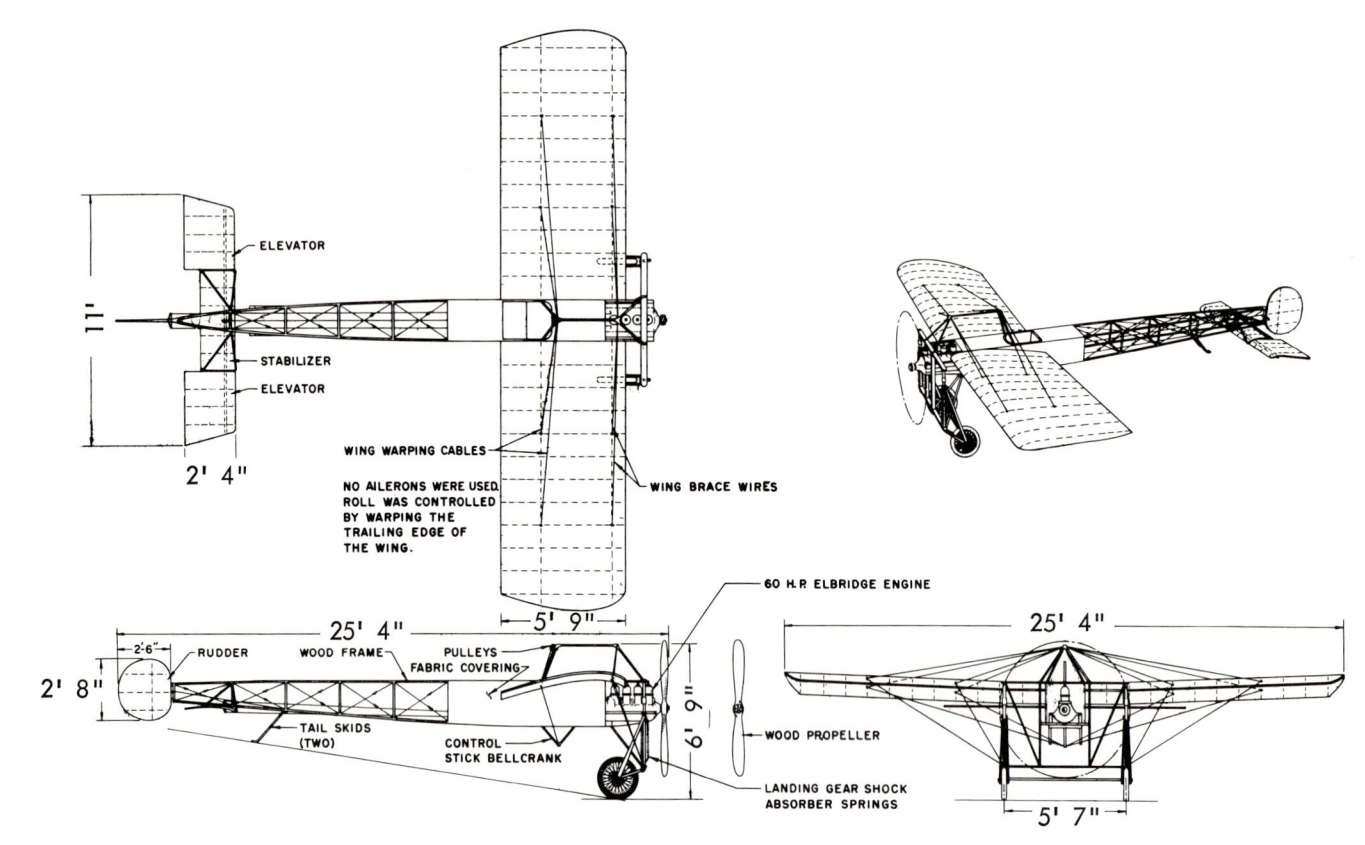

1911 Cessna

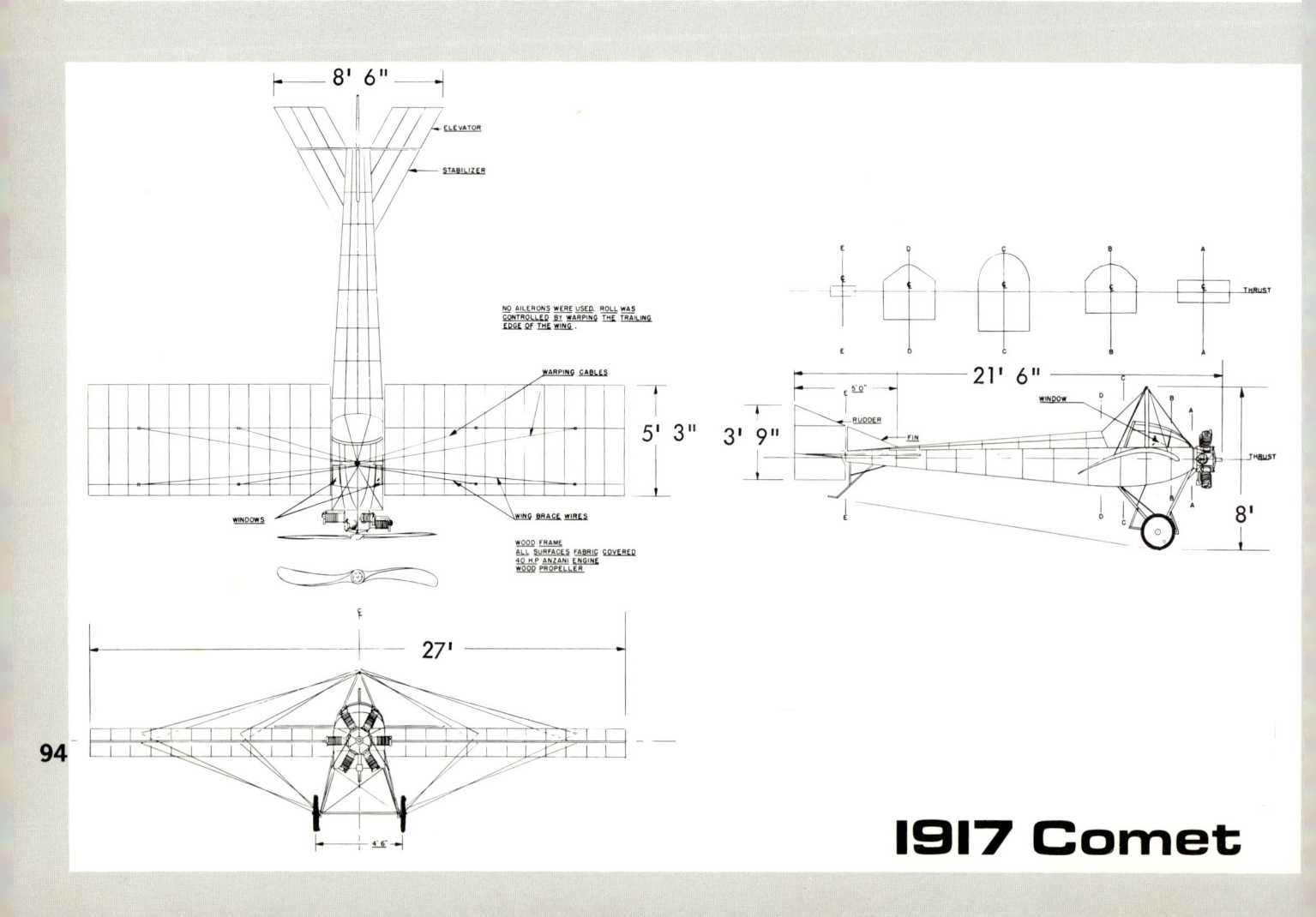

1917 Comet

Model AW

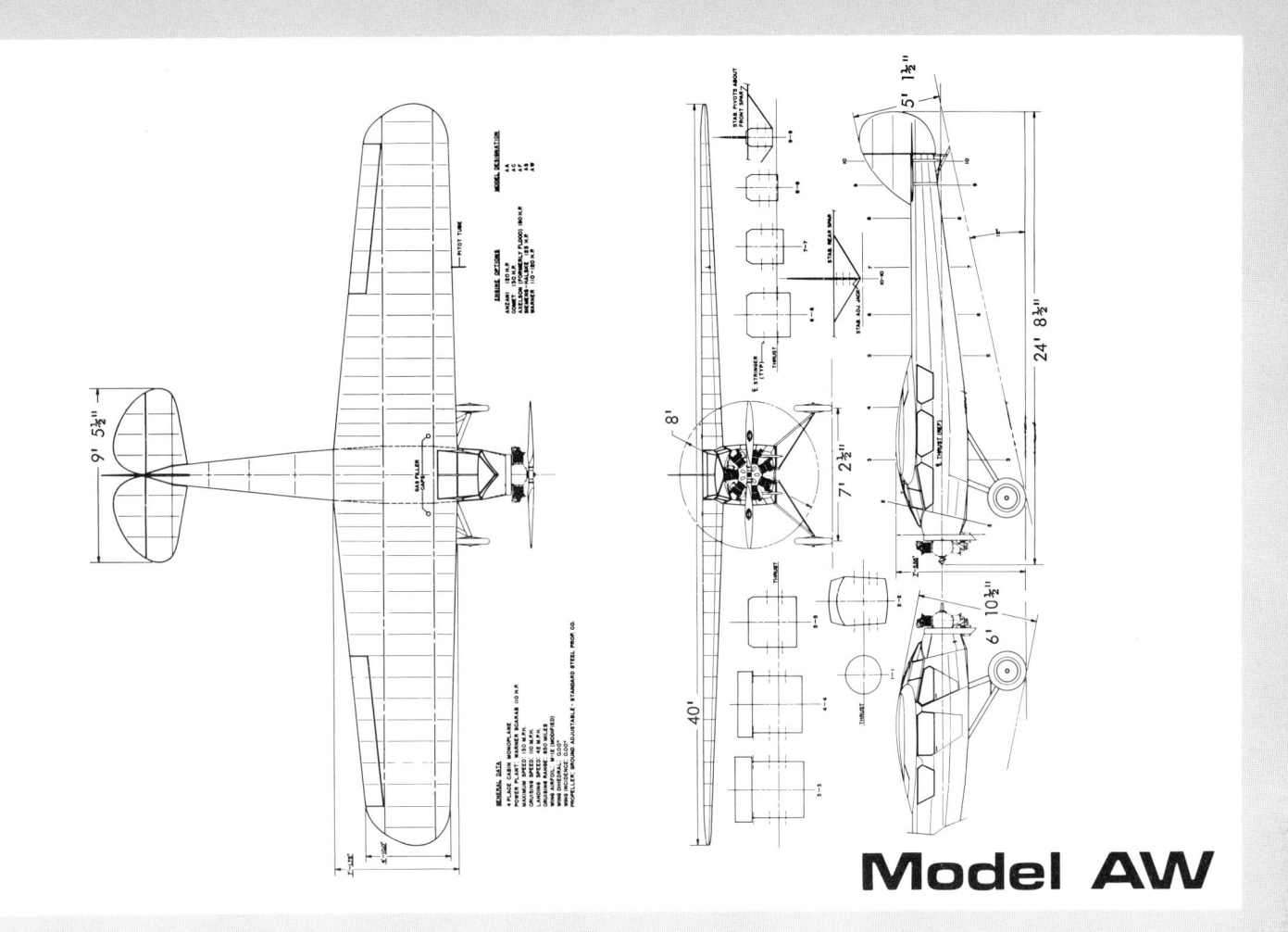

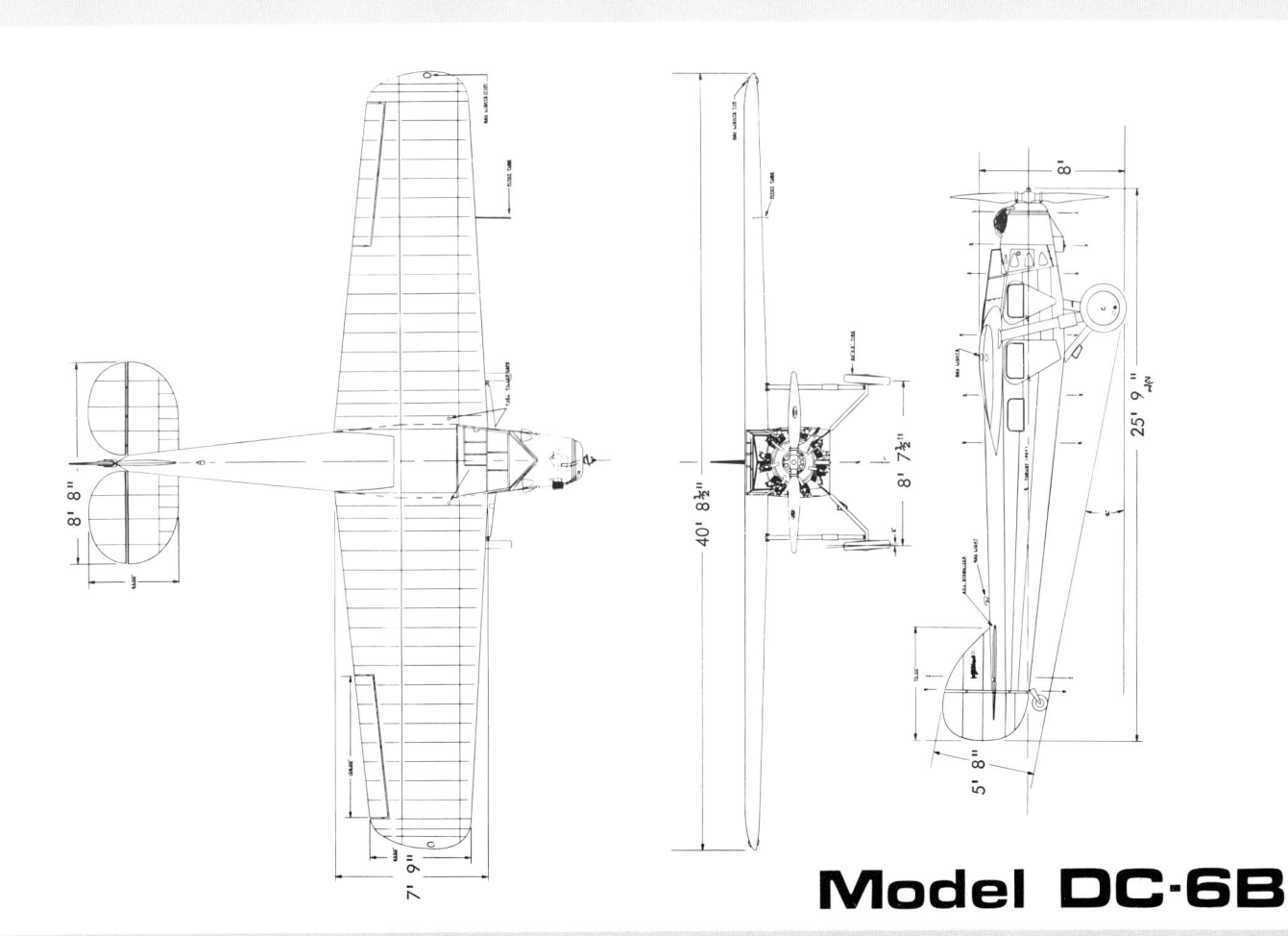

Model DC-6B

95

The Cessna Racers

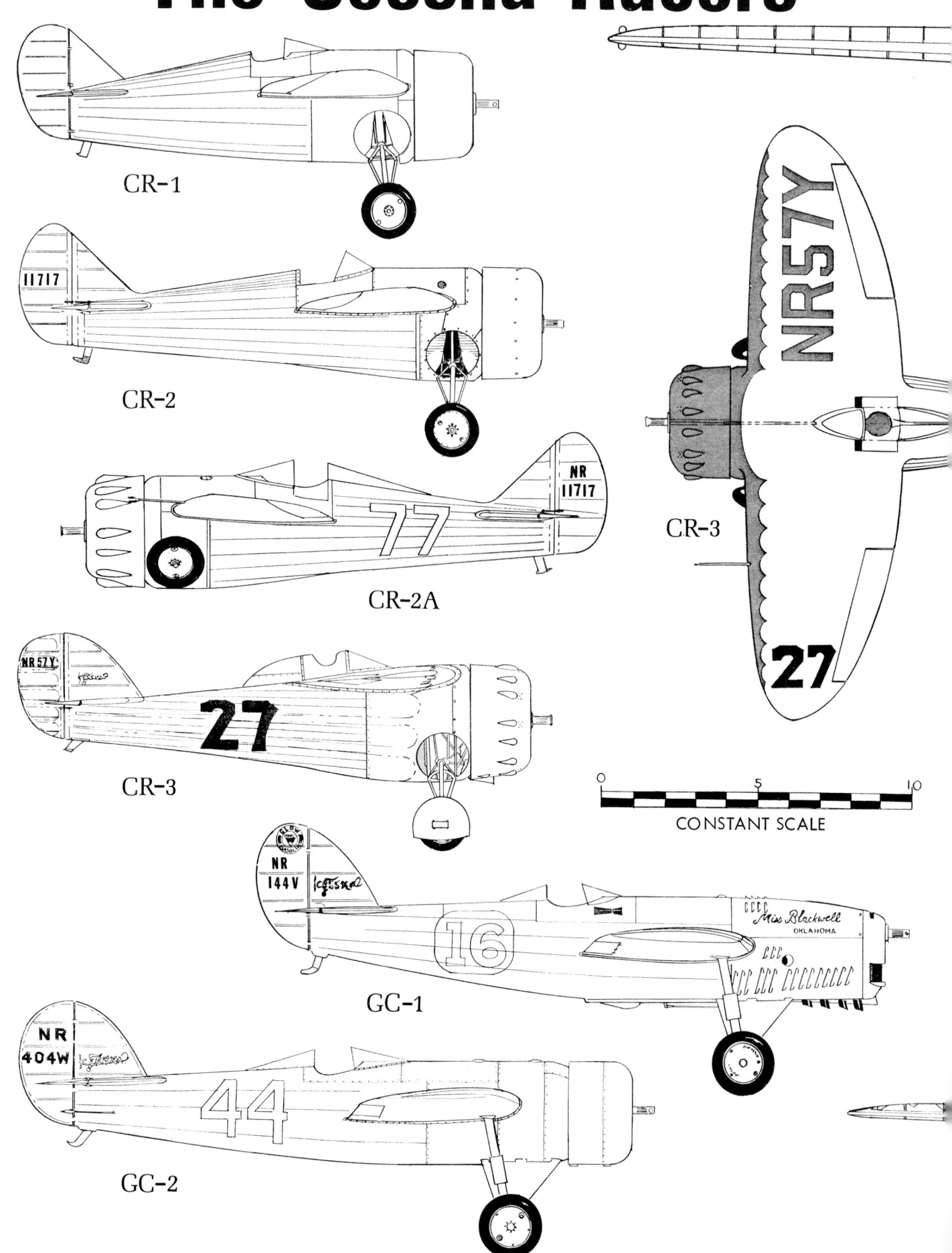

CR-1

CR-2

CR-2A

CR-3

CR-3

GC-1

GC-2

CONSTANT SCALE

CPW-6

CR-2

AW

MW-1

CPW-6

GC-2

Cessna Racer drawings on these two pages are adapted from artwork provided by Robert S. Hirsch, 8439 Dale St., Buena Park, CA. 90620. 5-view sets may be purchased from him.

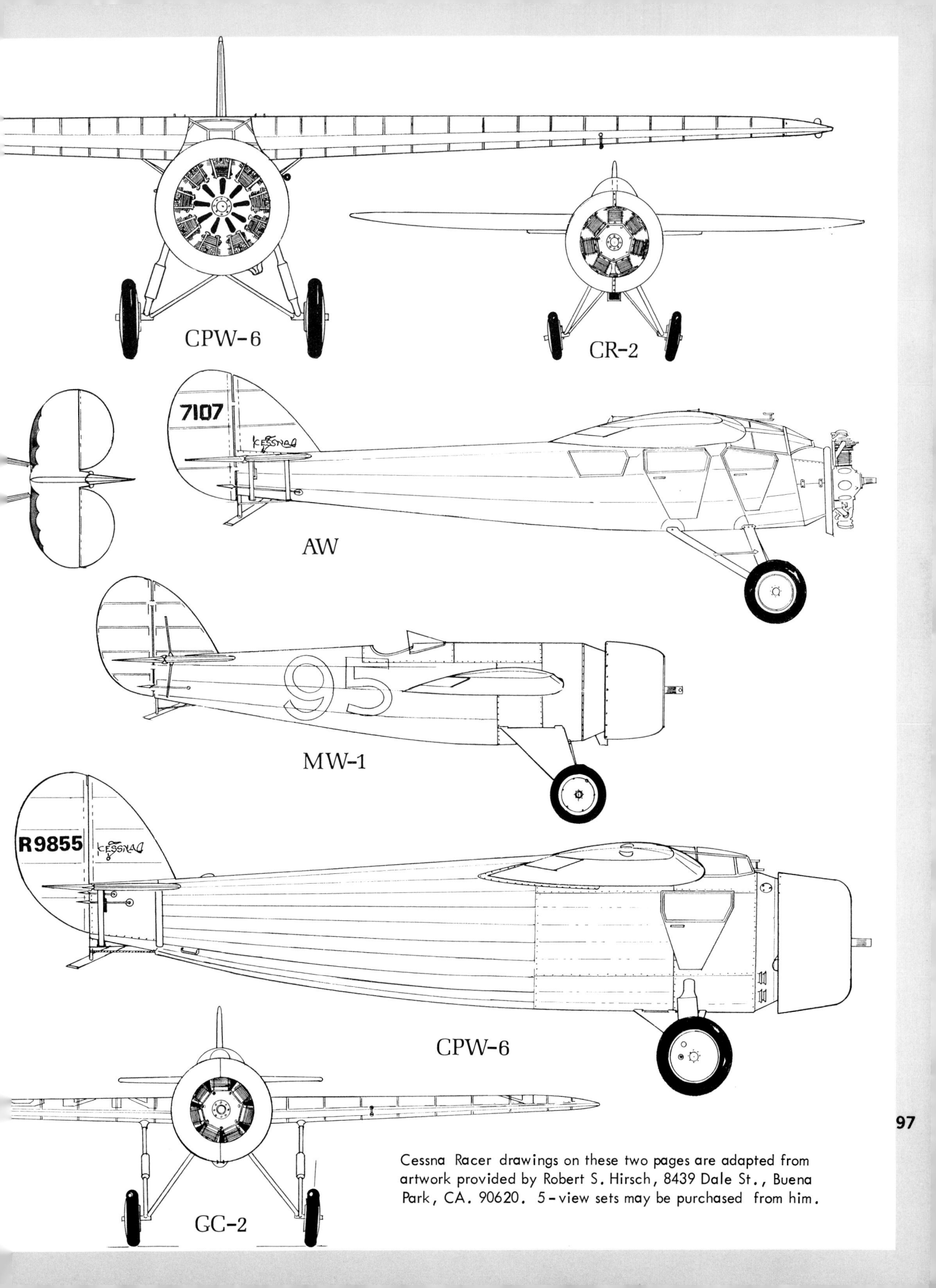

EXPLODED VIEW C-165

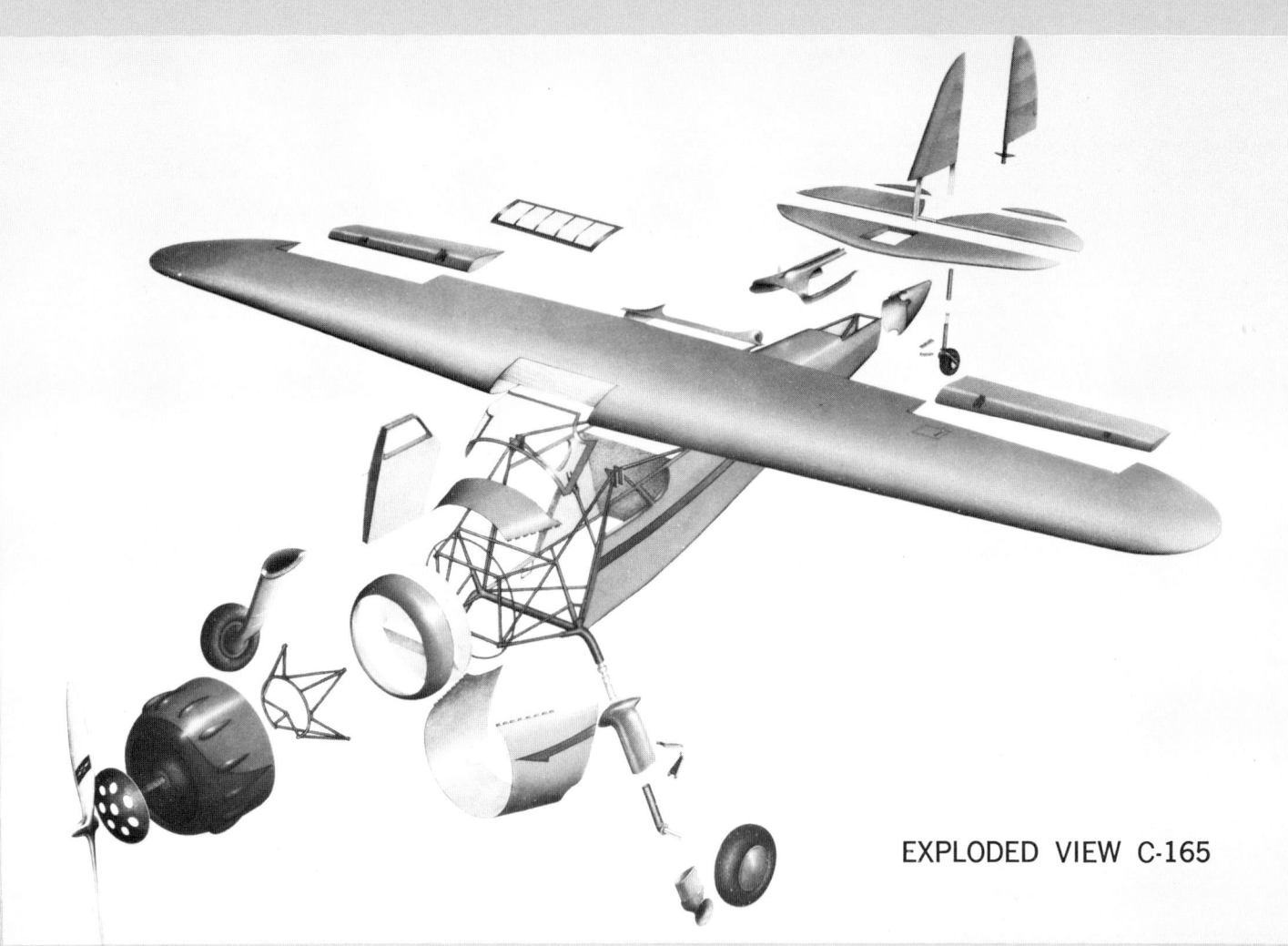

GENERAL DATA

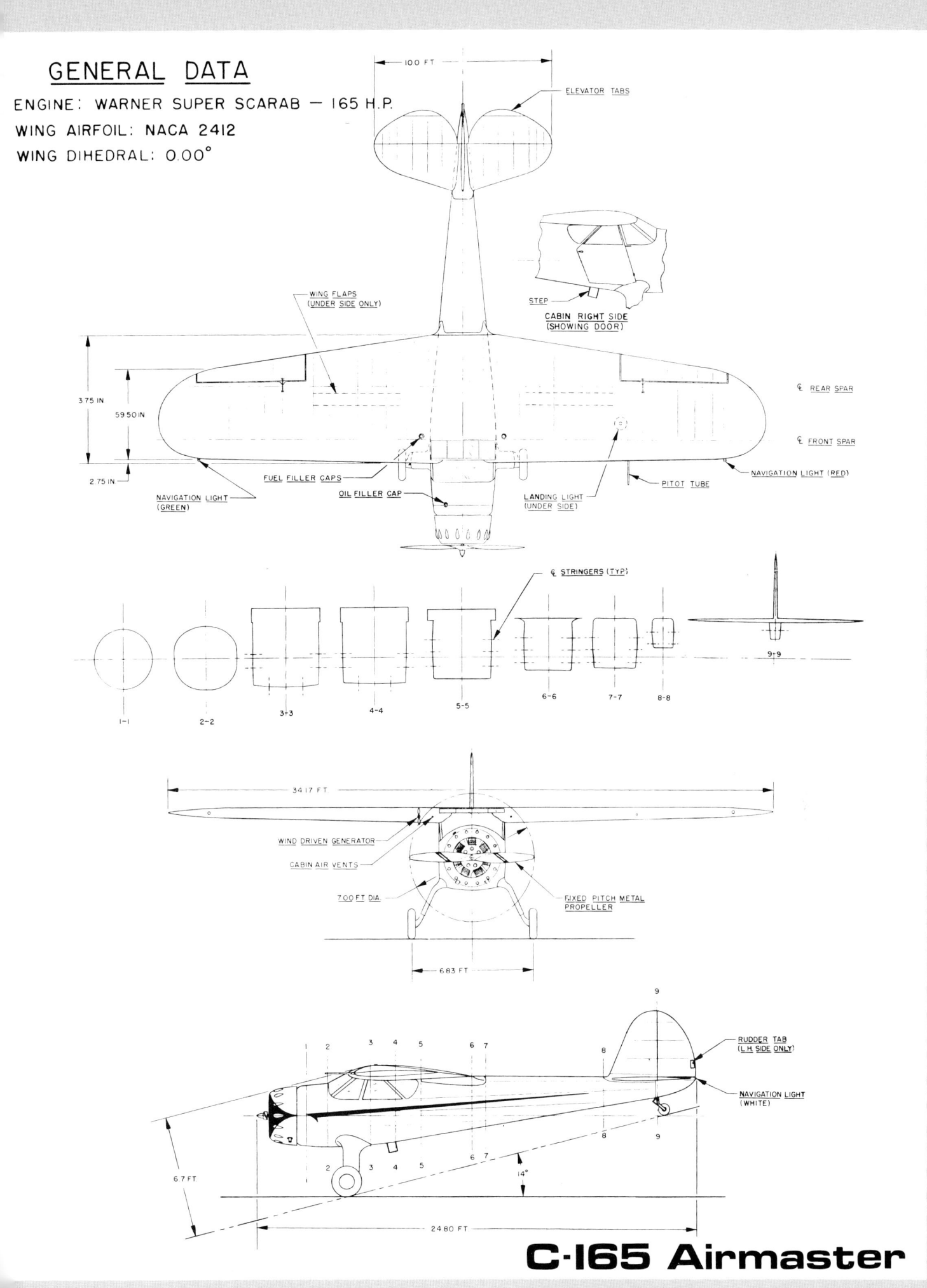

ENGINE: WARNER SUPER SCARAB — 165 H.P.
WING AIRFOIL: NACA 2412
WING DIHEDRAL: 0.00°

C-165 Airmaster

CUT-AWAY VIEW T-50

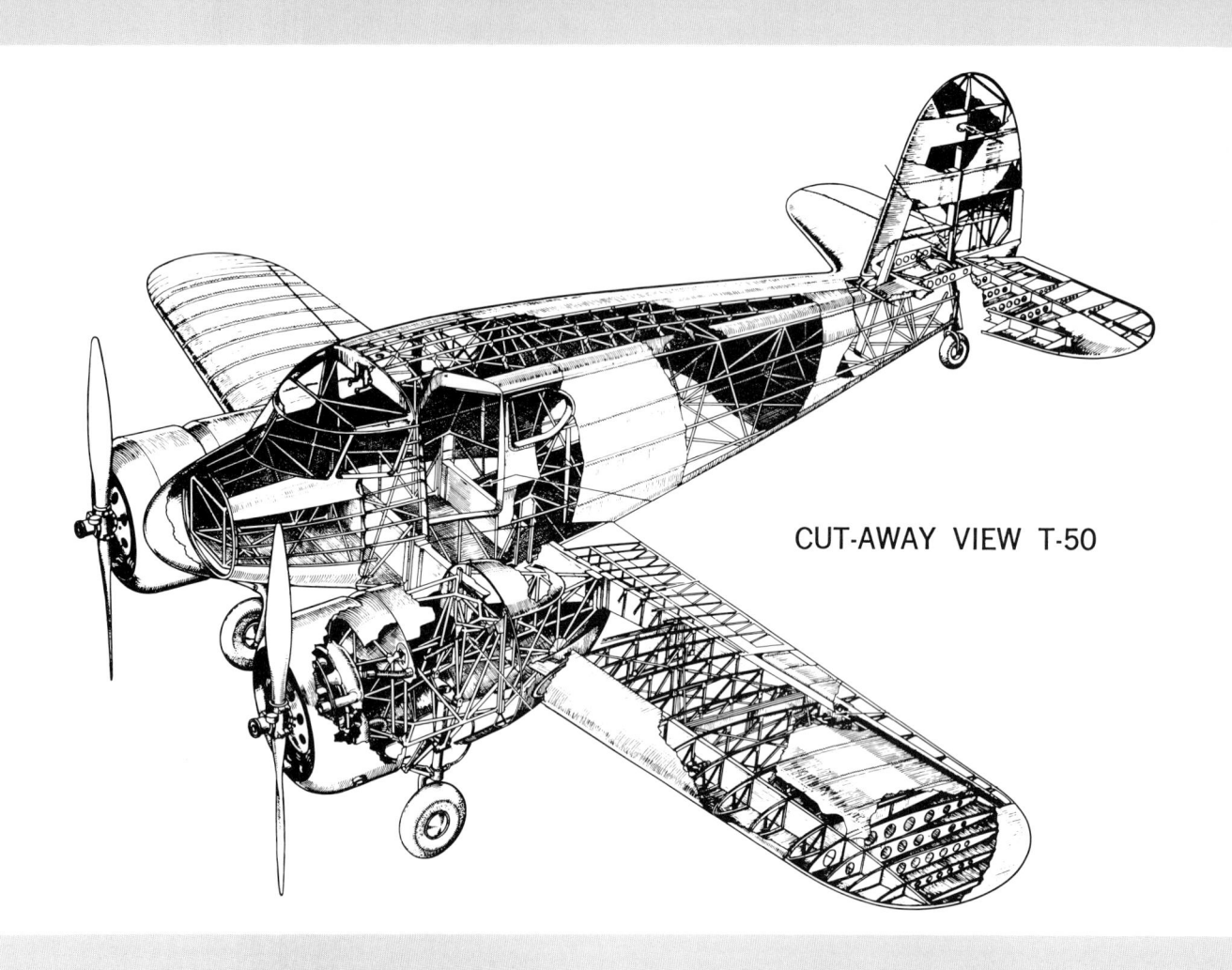

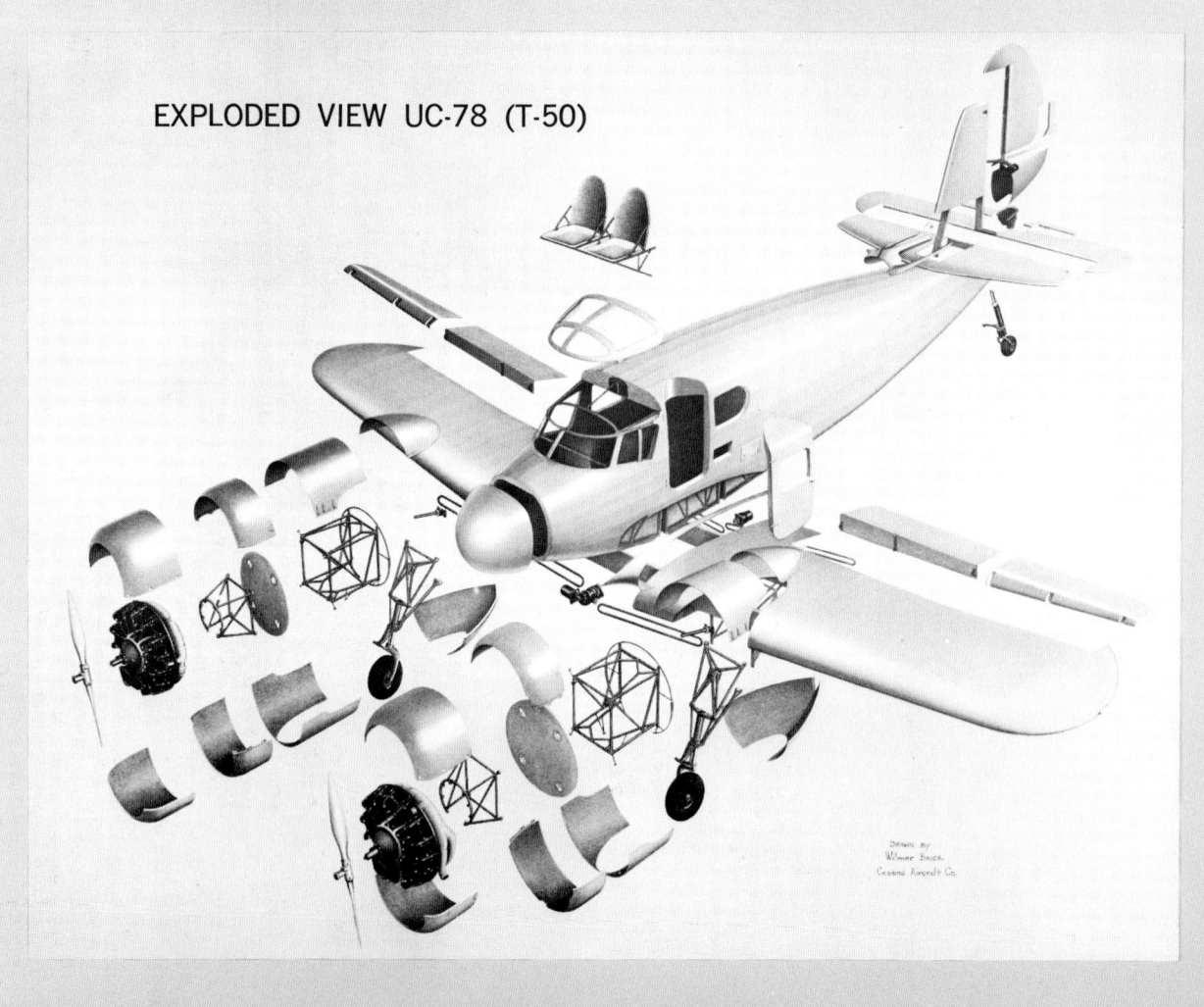

EXPLODED VIEW UC-78 (T-50)

UC-78 (T-50)

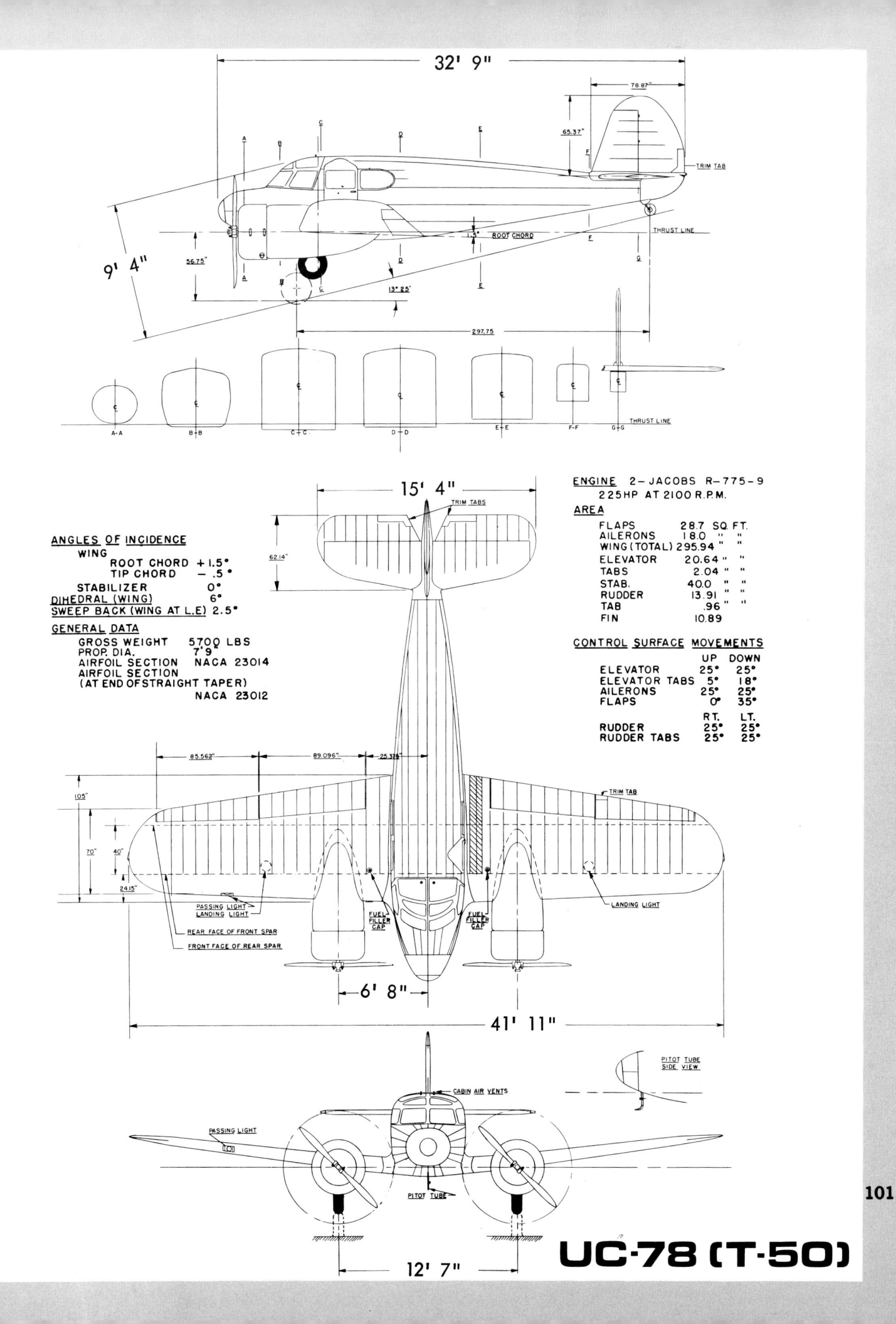

ANGLES OF INCIDENCE
- WING
  - ROOT CHORD +1.5°
  - TIP CHORD   −.5°
- STABILIZER   0°
- DIHEDRAL (WING)   6°
- SWEEP BACK (WING AT L.E.)   2.5°

GENERAL DATA
- GROSS WEIGHT   5700 LBS
- PROP. DIA.   7'9"
- AIRFOIL SECTION   NACA 23014
- AIRFOIL SECTION (AT END OF STRAIGHT TAPER)   NACA 23012

ENGINE 2-JACOBS R-775-9
225 HP AT 2100 R.P.M.

AREA
FLAPS	28.7 SQ. FT.
AILERONS	18.0 " "
WING (TOTAL)	295.94 " "
ELEVATOR	20.64 " "
TABS	2.04 " "
STAB.	40.0 " "
RUDDER	13.91 " "
TAB	.96 " "
FIN	10.89

CONTROL SURFACE MOVEMENTS

	UP	DOWN
ELEVATOR	25°	25°
ELEVATOR TABS	5°	18°
AILERONS	25°	25°
FLAPS	0°	35°

	RT.	LT.
RUDDER	25°	25°
RUDDER TABS	25°	25°

Dimensions: 32' 9" span; 9' 4"; 15' 4"; 6' 8"; 41' 11"; 12' 7"

140A

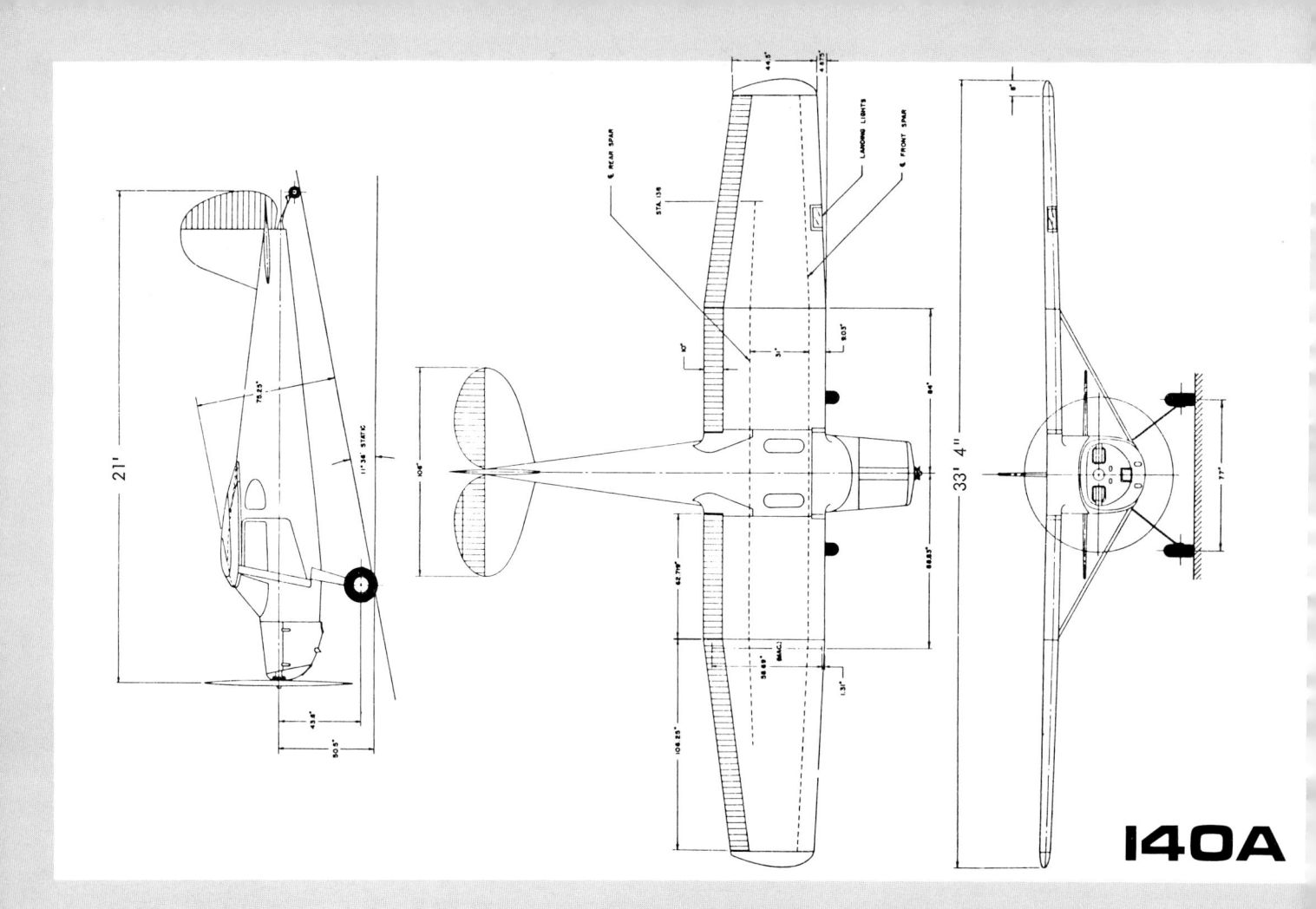

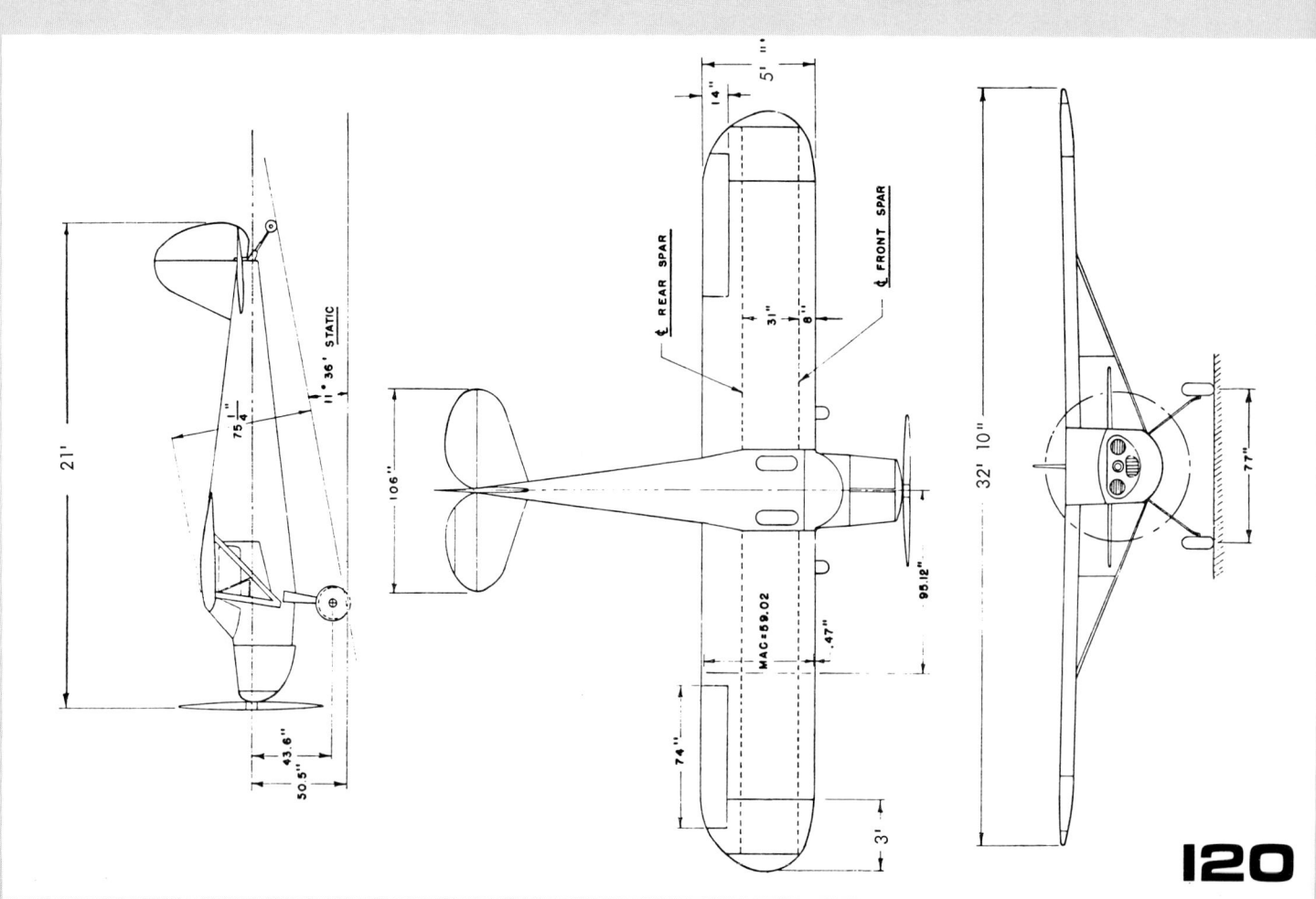

120

DESIGN EVOLUTION OF THE 150
External changes to the 150 shown as an aid to quick identification.

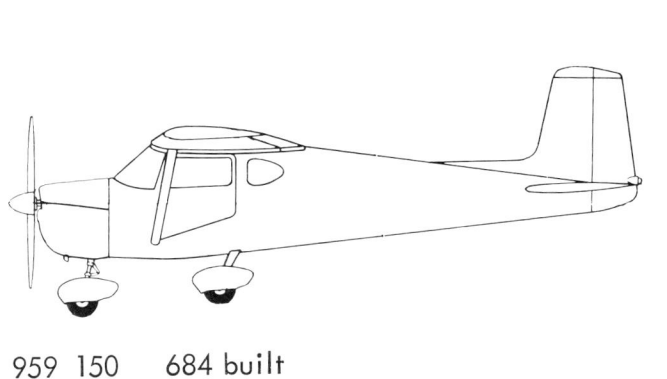

1959 150   684 built
1960 150   334 built

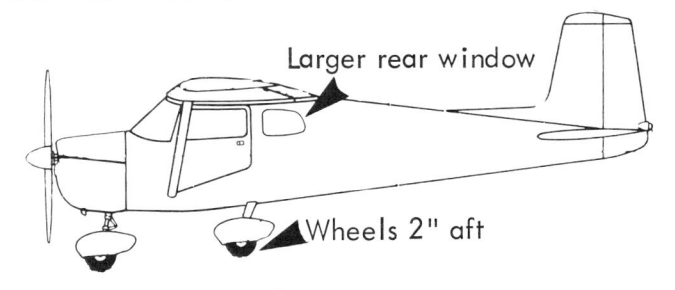

Larger rear window
Wheels 2" aft

1961 150A   333 built

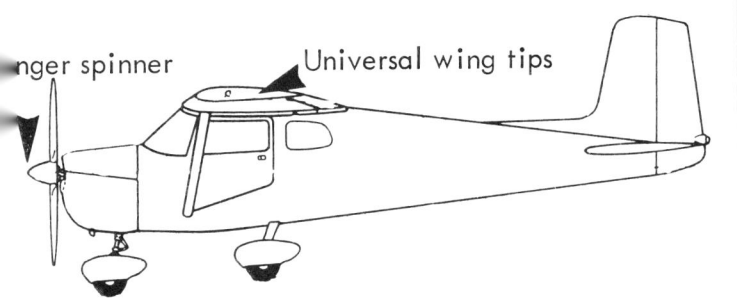

Longer spinner — Universal wing tips

1962 150B   350 built

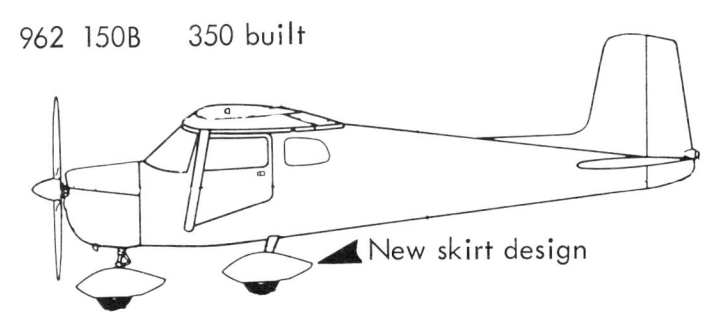

New skirt design

1963 150C   387 built

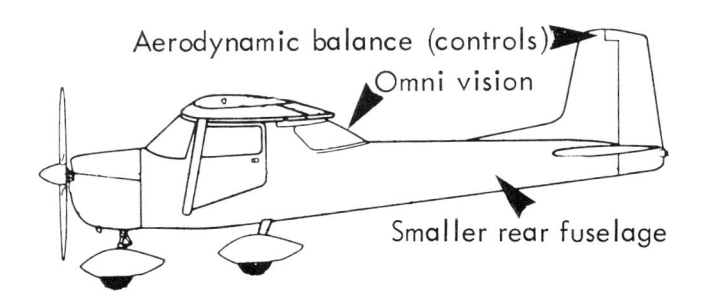

Aerodynamic balance (controls)
Omni vision
Smaller rear fuselage

1964 150D   686 built
1965 150E   760 built

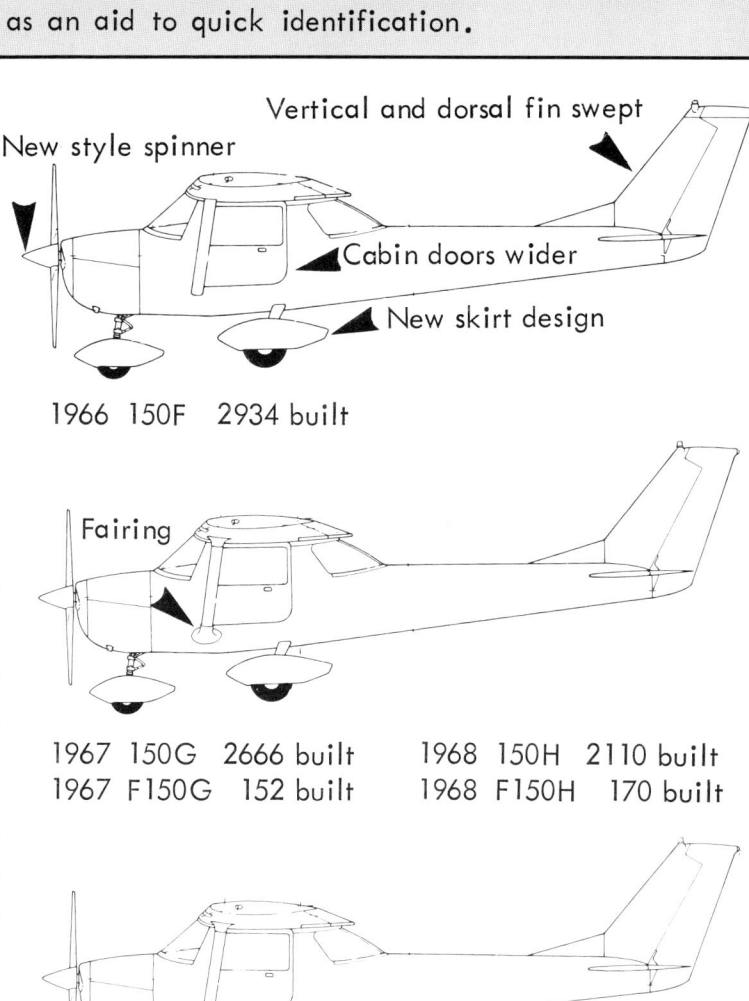

New style spinner
Vertical and dorsal fin swept
Cabin doors wider
New skirt design

1966 150F   2934 built

Fairing

1967 150G   2666 built   1968 150H   2110 built
1967 F150G   152 built   1968 F150H   170 built

New skirt design

1969 150J   1820 built
1969 F150J   140 built

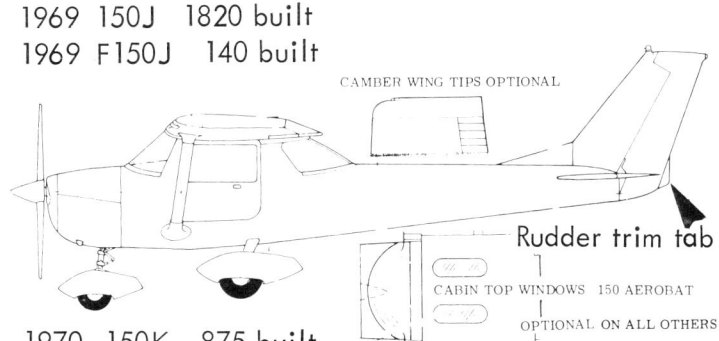

CAMBER WING TIPS OPTIONAL
Rudder trim tab
CABIN TOP WINDOWS 150 AEROBAT
OPTIONAL ON ALL OTHERS

1970 150K   875 built
1970 A150K   226 built   1970 FA150L   39 built
1970 F150K   129 built

Cowl lengthened
Dorsal fin lengthened
Tapered tubular gear
New skirt design
Landing light in nose

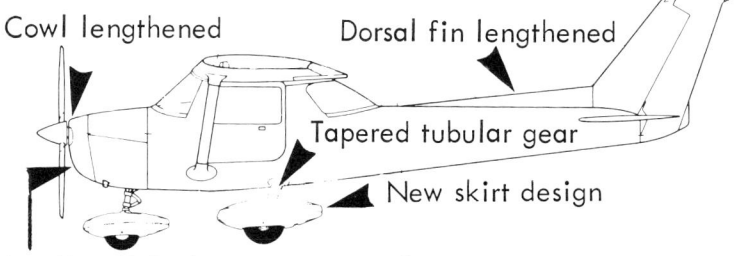

1971/1973   150L   2847 built
1971/1973   A150L   203 built
1971/1973   F150L   355 built
1971/1973   FRA150L   91 built

MODEL	NO. BUILT	YEARS	CLASS	ENGINE	WINGSPAN	LENGTH	HEIGHT	WT EMPTY	GR WT	VMX	VCR	RANGE
1911	No. Serial	1911	—	60 HP Elbridge	25'4''	25'4''	7'2''	—	—	—	—	—
1912	No Serial	1912	—	40 HP Anzani	25'4''	25'4''	7'2''	—	—	—	—	—
1913	No Serial	1913	—	40 Hp Anzani	25'4''	25'4'' Approx.	8'0''	—	—	—	—	—
1914	No Serial	1914	—	40 HP Anzani	25'4''	25'4''	8'0''	—	—	—	—	—
1915	No Serial	1915	—	60 HP Elbridge	25'4''	25'4''	8'0''	—	—	—	—	—
1916	No Serial	1916	—	40 HP Anzani	27'0	21'6''	8'0''	—	—	—	—	—
Comet	No Serial	1917	—	40 HP Anzani	27'0	21'6''	8'0''	—	—	124+	—	—
1926	No Serial	1926	4 PCLM	120 HP	—	—	—	—	—	—	—	—
Design No. 1	1	1927	3PLM	90 HP Anzani	25'	—	—	—	—	—	—	—
Design No. 2	1	1927	3PCLM	200 HP Wright	40'2''	23'8½''	—	—	—	150	—	—
Design No. 2 modified	(1)	1928	3PCLM	120 HP Anzani	40'2''	25'6''	—	—	—	—	—	—
AA	14 + (1)	1928	4PCLM	120 HP Anzani	40'2''	25'6''	—	1304	2260	130	—	—
AC	1 C/N 150	1928	4PCLM	130 HP Comet	40'2''	25'5''	—	—	2260	—	—	—
AF	3	1928	4PCLM	150 HP Axelson	40'2''	24'10½''	—	1554	2260	—	—	—
AS	3 + (1)	1928	4PCLM	125 HP Siem.-Halsk	40'2''	25'2¼''	7'5½''	—	2260	—	—	650
AW	48	1929-1930	4PCLM	110 HP Warner	40'2''	24'8½''	7'5½''	1225	2260	130	110	650
BW	13	1928	3 PCLM	220 HP Wright J-5	40'2''	25'10½''	—	—	2435	150	—	—
CW-6	1 C/N 146	1928	6 PCLM	220 HP Wright J-5	43'4''	30'4''	8'2''	2175	3950	148	120	610
DC-6	5	1929	4 PCLM	170 HP Curtiss	40'8½''	27'11''	7'8''	1767	2988	130	105	600
DC-6A	22	1929-30	4 PCLM	300 HP Wright	40'8½''	27'11½''	7'8''	1932	3180	161	130	650
DC-6B	22	1929-35	4 PCLM	225 HP Wright	40'8½''	28'0½''	7'8''	1871	3100	147	120	720
CG-1	1	1930	SPG	N/A	—	—	—	—	—	—	—	—
CG-2	84	1930	SPG	N/A	35'2''	18'	6'10''	—	—	—	—	—
CS-1	1	1930	SPS	N/A	—	—	—	—	—	—	—	—
CPG-1	1 C/N 39	1930	SPPG*	10 HP Cleone	35'2''	18'	6'10''	—	—	—	—	—
Baby Cessna	1 C/N 77	1930	1PCLM	25 HP Cleone	35'2''	18'±	—	—	—	—	—	—
EC-1	3	1930	1PCLM	25 HP Cleone	35'2''	18'±	—	—	—	—	—	—
EC-2	2	1930	2PCLM	30 HP E-107A	—	—	—	—	—	—	—	—
FC-1	1 C/N 248	1930	2PCLM	95 HP Cirrus	—	—	—	—	—	—	—	—
CPW-6	1 C/N 190	1929	Racer	Wasp	43'0''	30'3⅜''	8'2''	—	4250	160	130	—
GC-1	1 C/N 249	1930	1 Place Racer	90 HP Cirrus	27'0''	21'0''	—	—	1450	—	—	—
GC-2	1 C/N 252	1930	1 Place Racer	110 HP Warner	27'0''	20'5''	—	—	—	—	—	—

NOTES: ( ) Indicates number of aircraft "modified" from previous aircraft. c/n is "construction" number or "serial" number. SPG is Single Place Glider. SPS is Single Place Sailplane. SPPG is Single Place Powered Glider. Other abbreviations follow accepted FAA terminology. Gr Wt is Maximum Gross Take-off weight. VMx is Maximum Cruise Speed. VCr is Normal Cruise Speed.

Only known flight view of the CW-6 (c/n 146).

Another rare flight shot, the P-10.

Pioneer Tires BW (c/n 135) and others.

New York to Nome AW (c/n 140) NC7107.

Bare bones shows structure of 1928 AW.

AW (c/n 140) -Evan S. Prichard

Prototype C-37 (c/n 330) 1949. Bowers

C-165 GM Special (c/n 568) first version.

MODEL	NO. BUILT	YEARS	CLASS	ENGINE	WINGSPAN	LENGTH	HEIGHT	WT EMPTY	GR WEIGHT	VMX	VCR	RANGE
MW-1	1 C/N 195	1929	1 Place Racer	225 HP Wright J-5	36'0''	—	—	—	—	—	—	—
CR-1	1 CV Cessna	1932	1 Place Racer	125 HP Warner	18'6''	14'6''	—	—	—	176	—	—
CR-2	1 CV Cessna	1933	1 Place Racer	145 HP Warner	18'6''	17'0''	—	—	—	203	—	—
CR-3	1 CV Cessna	1933	1 Place Racer	145 HP Warner	18'6''	17'0''	—	—	750	255	—	—
C-3	1 CV Cessna	1933	4PCLM	125 HP Warner	—	—	—	—	2280	—	—	—
C-34	42	1935-36	4PCLM	145 HP Scarab	34'2''	24'8''	7'	1380	2350	162	143	535
C-37	46	1937	4PCLM	145 HP Warner	34'2''	24'8''	7'	1380	2350	162	143	525
C-38	16	1938	4PCLM	145 HP Warner	34'2''	24'8''	7'	1380	2350	162	151	525
C-145	42	1938-1940	4PCLM	145 HP Warner	34'2''	24'8''	7'	1380	2350	162	151	525
C-165	34	1939-41	4PCLM	165 HP Warner	34'2''	24'8''	7'	1400	2350	165	157	485
C-165D	3	1941	4PCLM	175 HP Warner	34'2''	24'8''	7'	—	2350	—	—	—
C-165 GM Spec.	1 C/N 586	1940	Exper. 4PCLM	175 HP GM X-250	34'2''	26'	7'	—	2350	—	—	—
T-50	40	1940-42	5PCLM	(2) 225 HP Jacobs	41'11''	32'9''	9'11''	3500	5100	191	175	750
AT-8	33	1941	5PCLM (Trainer)	(2) 225 HP Lyc R-680	41'11''	32'9''	9'11''	3500	5100	191	175	750
Crane I	640	1942	5PCLM (Trainer)	(2) 225 HP Jacobs	41'11''	32'9''	9'11''	3500	5100	195	175	750
AT-17	450	1942	5PCLM (Trainer)	(2) 225 HP Jacobs	41'11''	32'9''	9'11''	3500	5700	195	175	750
AT-17A	41	1942	5PCLM (Trainer)	(2) 225 HP Jacobs	41'11''	32'9''	9'11''	3500	5700	195	175	750
Crane Ia	182	1942	5PCLM (Trainer)	(2) 225 HP Jacobs	41'11''	32'9''	9'11''	3500	5700	195	175	750
AT-17B	466	1942	5PCLM Trainer	(2) 225 HP Jacobs	41'11''	32'9''	9'11''	3500	5700	195	175	750
AT-17C	60	1942	5PCLM (Trainer)	(2) 225 HP Jacobs	41'11''	32'9''	9'11''	3500	5700	195	175	750
AT-17D	131	1942	5PCLM (Trainer)	(2) 225 HP Jacobs	41'11''	32'9''	9'11''	3500	5700	195	175	750
AT-17E	Formerly AT-17	—	5PCLM (Trainer)	(2) 225 HP Jacobs	41'11''	32'9''	9'11''	3500	5300	195	175	750
UC-78E	Formerly UC-78B	—	5PCLM	(2) 225 HP Jacobs	41'11''	32'9''	9'11''	3500	5300	195	175	750
UC-78F	Formerly UC-78C	—	5PCLM	(2) 225 HP Jacobs	41'11''	32'9''	9'11''	3500	5300	195	175	750
JRC-1	(67) from AAF	—	5PCLM Utility	(2) 225 HP Jacobs	41'11''	32'9''	9'11''	3500	5700	195	175	750
T-50A	1 C/N P-7	1941	5PCLM Trainer	(2) 300 HP Jacobs	41'11''	32'9''	9'11''	3500	5100	—	—	—
P-10	1 C/N P-10	1941	2PCLM Trainer	(2) 300 HP Jacobs	—	—	—	—	—	—	—	—
C-106	1 C/N 10001	1943	2 Crew Cargo	(2) 550 HP P & W	64'8''	51'2''	11'4½''	9000	14000	195	170	830
C-106A	1 C/N 10002	1943	Crew Cargo	(2) 550 HP P & W	64'8''	51'2''	11'4½''	9000	14000	195	170	830
120	2172	1946/49	2PCLM	Cont. C-85-12	32'10''	21'6''	6'3¼''	785	1450	120	105	470
140	4904	1945/49	2PCLM	C-85-12 or C-90-12	32'10''	21'6''	6'3¼''	785	1450	120	105	470
140A	525	1949/51	2PCLM	C-85-12 or C-90-12	33'4''	21'6''	6'3¼''	900	1500	120	105	450

BW "Red Wing" 1929 -E. Prichard

Modern replica of 1912 Silver Wings

CS-1 sailplane (c/n 18) in flight, 1930.

AA "cantilever wing" test, February 2, 1928.

Only known full view of only C-3, NC12568.

Hand launching CG-2 glider, Feb. 5, 1930.

Float version of the CG-2 glider.

Rolling out the CR-2 racer.

150 SPECIFICATIONS

MODEL YEAR	MODEL	No. BUILT & CONSTRUCTION NUMBERS	PRICE	ENGINE	SPAN	LENGTH	HEIGHT	EMPTY WEIGHT	GROSS WEIGHT	VMx	VCr	RANGE
1959	150	684 (c/n 617 and 17001-17683)	$8545 (1)	Continental O-200A 100 hp	33'4"	21'11"	6'11"	962	1500	124	121	630
1960	150	334 (c/n 17684-17999, 59001-59018)	$8795 (1)	Continental O-200A 100 hp	33'4"	21'11"	6'11"	962	1500	124	121	630
1961	150A	333 (c/n 628 and 15059019-15059350)	$8995 (1)	Continental O-200A 100 hp	33'4"	21'11"	6'11"	950	1500	124	121	630
1962	150B	350 (c/n 15059351-15059700)	$8995 (1)	Continental O-200A 100 hp	33'6"	22'	6'11"	950	1500	127	125	610
1963	150C	387 (c/n 15059701-15060087)	$9435 (1)	Continental O-200A 100 hp	33'6"	22'	6'11"	950	1500	127	125	610
1964	150D	686 (c/n 644 and 15060088-15060772)	$9495 (1)	Continental O-200A 100 hp	33'6"	22'	6'11"	1010	1600	125	122	565
1965	150E	760 (c/n 15060773-15061532)	$9425 (1)	Continental O-200A 100 hp	33'6"	22'	6'11"	1010	1600	125	122	565
1966	150F (note 2)	2934 (c/n 649 and 15061533-15064532)	$9275 (1)	Continental O-200A 100 hp	32'8½"	23'9"	8'5"	1060	1600	125	122	565
1966	F150F	67 (c/n F15000001-F15000067)	-	Rolls Royce O-200A 100 hp	32'8½"	23'9"	8'5"	1060	1600	125	122	565
1967	150G	2666 (c/n 15064533-15067198)	$9550 (1)	Continental O-200A 100 hp	32'8½"	23'9"	8'5"	1060	1600	125	122	565
1967	F150G	152 (c/n F15000068-F15000219)	-	Rolls Royce O-200A 100 hp	32'8½"	23'9"	8'5"	1060	1600	125	122	565
1968	150H	2110 (c/n 15067199-15069308)	$10,195	Continental O-200A 100 hp	32'8½"	23'9"	8'5"	1060	1600	122	117	565
1968	F150H	170 (c/n F15000220-F15000389)	-	Rolls Royce O-200A 100 hp	32'8½"	23'9"	8'5"	1060	1600	122	117	565
1969	150J	1820 (c/n 15069309-15071128)	$10,995 (1)	Continental O-200A 100 hp	32'8½"	23'9"	8'5"	1060	1600	122	117	565
1969	F150J	140 (c/n F15000390-F15000529)	-	Rolls Royce O-200A 100 hp	32'8½"	23'9"	8'5"	1060	1600	122	117	565
1970	150K	875 (c/n 15071129-15072003)	$11,450 (1)	Continental O-200A 100 hp	33'2"	23'9"	8'5"	1060	1600	122	117	565
1970	A150K	226 (c/n A1500001-A1500226)	$10,495	Continental O-200A 100 hp	33'2"	23'9"	8'5"	1040	1600	120	115	555
1970	F-150K	129 (c/n F15000530-F15000658)	-	Rolls Royce O-200A 100 hp	33'2"	23'9"	8'5"	1060	1600	122	117	565
1970	FA150K	81 (c/n FA1500001-FA1500081)	-	Rolls Royce O-200A 100 hp	33'2"	23'9"	8'5"	1040	1600	120	115	555
1971-1974	150L	3739 (c/n 15072004-15075781) ◄ note 3 ►	$11,995 $12,550	Continental O-200A 100 hp	33'2"	23'8½"	7'9½"	1060	1600	122	117	565
1971-1974	A150L	288 (c/n A1500227-A1500523) ◄ note 4 ►	$10,995 $11,595	Continental O-200A 100 hp	33'2"	23'8½"	7'9½"	note 5	1600	120	115	555
1972-1975	A-150L note 6	37 (c/n A-1501001-A-1501037)	-	Continental O-200A 100 hp	33'2"	23'8½"	7'9½"	1060	1600	122	117	565
1972-1975	A-A150L	9 (c/n A-A1500001-A-A1500009) note 7	-	Continental O-200A 100 hp	33'2"	23'8½"	7'9½"	note 8	1600	120	115	555
1971-1974	F150L	485 (c/n F15000659-15001143)	$10,995	Rolls Royce O-200A 100 hp	33'2"	23'8½"	7'9½"	1060	1600	122	117	565
1971	FA150L	39 (c/n FA1500082-FA1500120)	$13,295	Rolls Royce O-200A 100 hp	33'2"	23'8½"	7'9½"	1030	1600	120	115	555
1972-1974	FRA150L	141 (c/n FA1500121-FA1500261)	-	Rolls Royce O-240A 130 hp	33'2"	23'8½"	7'9½"	-	1650	-	-	-
1975-1976	150M	1224 (c/n 15075782-15077005 - note 9)	$16,925 note 10	Continental O-200A 100 hp	33'2"	23'11"	8'3½"	note 11	1600	125	122	660
1975-1976	A150M	86 (c/n A1500524-A1500609 - note 12)	$13,325 note 13	Continental O-200A 100 hp	33'2"	23'11"	8'3½"	note 14	1600	124	121	650
1975-1976	F150M	105 (c/n F15001144-F15001248 - note 15)	-	Rolls Royce O-200A 100 hp	33'2"	23'11"	8'3½"	note 16	1600	125	122	660
1975-1976	FRA150M	20 (c/n FA1500262-FA1500281 - note 17)	-	Rolls Royce O-240A 130 hp	33'2"	23'11"	8'3½"	-	1600	-	-	-

----

NOTE 1 - Price is for basic "Commuter" model. NOTE 2 - 67 F150 are included in this block of c/n and have additional French numbers. NOTE 3 - 39 Argentine A-150L are included in this block of c/n and have additional Argentine numbers. More NOTE 3, price was $11,995 for Commuter in 1971, $12,550 for Commuter in 1972, 1973, 1974. NOTE 4 - 9 Argentine A-A150 are included in this block of c/n and have additional Argentine numbers. Price for Commuter model was $10,995 in 1971, $11,595 in 1973 thru 1974. NOTE 5 - Empty weight was 1030 in 1971, 1035 in 1972, 1040 in 1973-1974. NOTE 6 - There were 18 A-150L built in 1972, 15 in 1973, none in 1974 and 4 in 1975. NOTE 7 - There were 6 A-A150L built in 1972 and 3 built in 1973, none in 1974 or 1975. NOTE 8 - Empty weight of A-A150L was 1035 in 1972 and 1040 in 1973. NOTE 9 - 1976 150M production started with c/n 1507706. NOTE 10 - Price for "Commuter II" was $16,925 in 1975 and $18,750 in 1976. NOTE 11 - Empty weight of 150M was 1065 in 1975 and 1122 in 1976. NOTE 12 - 1976 A150M production started with c/n A1500610. NOTE 13 - Price of A150M was $13,325 in 1975 and $15,250 in 1976. NOTE 14 - Empty weight of A150M was 1040 in 1975 and 1076 in 1976. NOTE 15 - 1976 F150M production started with c/n F15001249. NOTE 16 - Empty weight of F150M was 1065 in 1975 and 1122 in 1976. NOTE 17 - 1976 FRA150M production started with c/n FA1500282.

1928 AW showing door & cockpit.

DC-6B instrument panel (June 7, 1929).

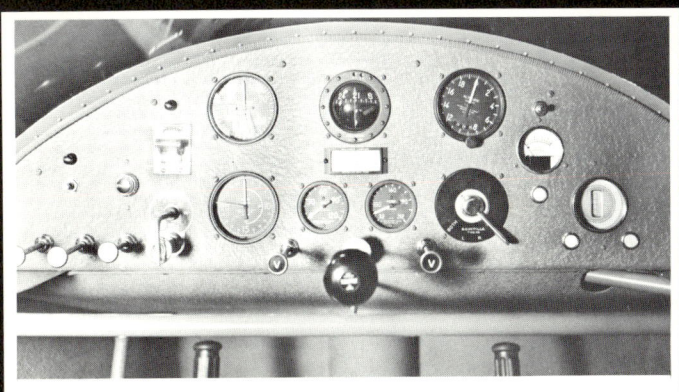

C-37 Airmaster instruments (Jan 22, 1937).

1939 C-145 panel (Sept. 11, 1938).

C-165 instruments (July 1, 1939).

T-50 (c/n 1001) NC27299 (March 30, 1940).

AT-17 (c/n 1701) AAF 42-002.

1966 150F instrument panel.

PRE-WAR AIRCRAFT
Production in C/N Sequence

C/N	MODEL	REGISTRATION (Prefix Left Off)
112	AA	4165
113	BW	4158
114	AA	4156
115	AS	4157
116	BW	5834
117	BW	5835
118	BW	4724
119	AA	5036
120	BW	4725
121	BW	5035
122	AA	5034
123	AS	5333
124	AA	5335
125	BW	5336
126	AA	5579
127	AA	5580
128	AA	5581
129	AA	5582
130	AA	5583
131	AA	5584
132	AA	5585
133	AA	5586
134	AA	5587
135	BW	6623
136	AS	6624
137	AF	6625
138	BW	6442
139	AS	'?'
140	AW	7107
141	AF	7462
142	BW	6441
143	AA	6443
144	BW	6444
145	AW	6445
146	CW-6	6446
147	BW	6447
148	AW	6448
149	AF	6449
150	AC	6450
151	AW	9091
152	AW	9092
153	AW	9093
154	AW	9094
155	AW	9095
156	AW	8141
157	DC-6	8142
158	AW	8143
159	AW	8144
160	AW	8145
161	AW	8146
162	AW	8147
163	AW	8148
164	AW	8149
165	AW	8150
166	AW	8781
167	AW	8782
168	AW	8783
169	AW	8784
170	AW	8785
171	AW	8786
172	AW	8787
173	AW	8788
174	AW	8789
175	AW	8790
176	AW	8791
177	AW	8792
178	AW	8793
179	AW	8794
180	AW	8795
181	AW	8796
182	AW	8797
183	AW	8798
184	AW	8799
185	AW	8800
186	AW	9851
187	AW	9852
188	AW	9853
189	AW	9854
190	CPW-6	9855
191	AW	9856
192	AW	9857
193	AW	9858
194	AW	9859
195	MW-1	9860
196	AW	9861
197	AW	9862
198	DC-6B	9863
199	DC-6A	9864
200	DC-6	9865
201	DC-6B	9866
202	DC-6	9867
203	DC-6	9868
204	DC-6A	9869
205	DC-6B	637K
206	DC-6A	627K
207	DC-6A	635K
208	DC-6A	636K
209	DC-6A	638K
210	DC-6B	9870
211	DC-6B	631K
212	DC-6B	630K
213	DC-6	634K
214	DC-6B	632K
215	DC-6B	639K
216	DC-6B	644K
217	DC-6B	629K
218	DC-6B	628K
219	DC-6B	633K
220	DC-6B	641K
221	DC-6B	643K
222	DC-6B	642K
223	DC-6B	6444
224		?
225	DC-6A	655K
226	DC-6A	6441
227	DC-6A	640K
228	DC-6A	651K
229	DC-6A	652K
230	DC-6A	653K
231	DC-6A	6449
232	DC-6A	654K
233	DC-6A	301M
234	DC-6A	646K
235	DC-6A	647K
236	DC-6A	648K
237	DC-6A	300M
238	DC-6A	302M
239		?
240	DC-6B	303M
241	DC-6A	306M
242		?
243	AW	337M
244	DC-6B	305M
245	DC-6A	137V
246	DC-6B	145V
247		?
248	FC-1	138V
249	GC-1	144V
250	EC-1	403V
251	EC-2	403W
252	GC-2	404W
253	EC-2	405W
254	C-34	12599
255	C-34	14425 (1)
256/274		(Not Used ?)
275	DC-6B	569Y
276	DC-6B	59Y
277/289		(Not Used ?)
290	DC-6B	14452
291/299		(Not Used)
300	C-34	14460
301	C-34	15462
302	C-34	15463
303	C-34	15464
304	C-34	15465
305	C-34	15466
306	C-34	15467
307	C-34	15468
308	C-34	15469
309	C-34	15470
310	C-34	15471
311	C-34	15819
312	C-34	(Portugal)
313	C-34	R307 (2)
314	C-34	G-AEAI (3)
315	C-34	15821
316	C-34	15820
317	C-34	15850
318	C-34	15851
319	C-34	16409 (4)
320	C-34	15852 (5)
321	C-34	16402
322	C-34	16403
323	C-34	16404
324	C-34	16405
325	C-34	16406
326	C-34	16407
327	C-34	16408
328	C-34	16453
329	C-34	16452
330	C-37	17070
331	C-34	16454
332	C-34	16455
333	C-34	17050
334	C-34	17051
335	C-34	17052
336	C-34	(So Africa)
337	C-34	17054
338	C-34	17055
339	C-34	VH-UYG (6)
340	C-34	(So Africa)
341		?
342	C-37	17059
343	C-37	17053
344	C-37	17056
345	C-37	17057
346	C-37	17086
347	C-37	17087
348	C-37	17088
349	C-37	NPC-33 (7)
350	C-37	17090
351	C-37	17089
352	C-37	17058
353	C-37	NPC-34 (7)
354	C-37	CF-BFE (8)
355	C-37	18030
356	C-37	18031
357	C-37	VH-UZU (9)
358	C-37	18032
359	C-37	18033
360	C-37	18034
361	C-37	18035
362	C-37	18036
363	C-37	18037
364	C-37	18045
365	C-37	18046
366	C-37	18047
367	C-37	CR-IAC (17)
368	C-37	18049
369	C-37	18550
370	C-37	18551
371	C-37	18552
372	C-37	18553
373	C-37	18554
374	C-37	CF-BHB (10)
375	C-37	18590 (11)
376	C-37	18591
377	C-37	18592
378	C-37	18593
379	C-37	18594
380	C-37	18595
381	C-37	18596
382	C-37	18597
383	C-37	18598
384	C-37	18599
385	C-37	OH-VKF (12)
386	C-37	18589
387/399		(Not Used)
400	C-38	18048
401	C-38	18794
402	C-38	18795
403	C-38	18796
404	C-38	19460
405	C-38	18797
406	C-38	18798
407	C-38	18799
408	C-38	19455
409	C-38	19456
410	C-38	19457
411	C-38	19458
412	C-38	19459
413	C-38	19461
414	C-38	19462
415	C-38	19463
416/449		(Not Used)
450	C-145	19464
451	C-145	19465
452	C-145	PP-TEH (13)
453	C-145	19483
454	C-145	19484
455	C-145	19485
456	C-145	19486
457	C-145	19487
458	C-145	19488
459	C-145	19489
460	C-145	19490
461	C-145	19491
462	C-145	19478
463	C-145	19495
464	C-145	OH-YNB (14)
465	C-145	19496
466	C-165	19497
467	C-145	19498
468	C-145	19499
469	C-145	20781
470	C-145	20782
471	C-145	20783
472	C-145	4120
473	C-145	20759
474	C-145	20763
475	C-145	20761
476	C-145	20762
477	C-165	20760
478	C-165	20764
479	C-165	20765
480	C-145	20766
481	C-145	20767
482	C-165	20758
483	C-145	21907
484	C-145	113 (15)
485	C-145	114
486	C-145	21908
487		?
488	C-165	21910
489/549		(Not Used)
550	C-165	21909
551	C-165	21911
552	C-145	21912
553	C-145	21913
554	C-165	21914
555	C-165	21915
556	C-165	21916
557	C-165	21941
558	C-165	21942
559	C-165	21943
560	C-165	21944
561	C-165	21945
562	C-165	21946
563	C-165	21948
564	C-165	89Y
565	C-145	21949
566	C-145	25461
567	C-145	25462
568	C-165	25463 (16)
569	C-165	25464
570	C-145	25465
571	C-145	25466
572	C-165	25467
573	C-165	25468

C/N	Model	Reg
574	C-165	25469
575	C-165	25480
576	C-145	25481
577	C-165	25482
578	C-145	25483
579	C-165D	25484
580	C-165	25485
581	C-165	25486
582	C-145	25487
583	C-165	32450
584	C-165D	32451
585	C-145	32452
586	C-165D	32453
587	C-165	32454
588	C-165	32455
589	C-165	32457
590	C-165	21938
591	C-165	32458
592/599		Not Used
600-999 reserved for experimental		
1000	T-50	20784
1001	T-50	27299

C/N	Model	Reg
1002	T-50	21937
1003	T-50	34 (CAA)
1004	T-50	33 (CAA)
1005	T-50	4500
1006	T-50	35 (CAA)
1007	T-50	37 (CAA)
1008	T-50	4400
1009	T-50	21940
1010	T-50	3 (CAA)
1011	T-50	131 (CAA)
1012	T-50	1620
1014	T-50	1630
1015	T-50	132 (CAA)
1016	T-50	133 (CAA)
1017	T-50	5069
1018	T-50	21939
1019/1029		Not Used
1030/1062		See AT-8
1063/1099		Not Used
1100/1299		See Crane I
1300		Not Used
1301	T-50	25488

C/N	Model	Reg
1302	T-50	25489
1303	T-50	25490
1304	T-50	5069
1305A	T-50	32456
1306	T-50	12 (CAA)
1307	T-50	118 (CAA)
1308	T-50	4 (CAA)
1309	T-50	6 (CAA)
1310	T-50	7 (CAA)
1311	T-50	34752
1312	T-50	34753
1313		Not Built
1314	T-50	34754
1315	T-50	34755
1316	T-50	34756
1317	T-50	34757
1318	T-50	34758
1319	T-50	34759
1320	T-50	34760
1321	T-50	34761
1322	T-50	34762
1323	T-50	44500
1324/1349		Not Used

NOTES: (1) to Mexico as XB-AJO. (2) to Argentine Republic as LV-BDA. (3) Great Britain. (4) to Great Britain as G-AFBY, impressed into RAF as HM502. (5) to Canada as CF-BDI. (6) Australia, impressed into RAAF as s/n A40-1 during World War II, to VH-UYG and to VH-KWM in 1963. (7) Phillippines. (8) Canada. (9) Brazil. (10) Canada. (11) to Norway as LN-FAK. (12) Finland. (13) Brazil. (14) Finland. (15) c/n 485 and 485 were Civil Aeronautics Authority aircraft (USA). (16) General Motors Special. (17) Portugese West Africa.

MILITARY SERIAL from - thru	MODEL	QTY.	C/N	REGISTRATION	REMARKS
42-38290	UC-77	(1)	238	NC302M	DC-6A, impressed
42-38292	UC-77A	(1)	211	NC631K	DC-6B, impressed
42-38293	UC-77A	(1)	219	NC633K	DC-6B, impressed
42-38294	UC-77A	(1)	290	NC14452	DC-6B, impressed
42-38295	UC-77A	(1)	200	NC9865	DC-6B, impressed
42-46637	UC-77	(1)	232	NC654K	DC-6A, impressed
42-46638	UC-77	(1)	221	NC643K	DC-6A, impressed
42-46639	UC-77	(1)	226	NC6441	DC-6A, impressed
42-61101-61460	CG-4A	360	Unknown		Waco glider
42-61461-61820	CG-4A	-0-	Not built		Order Cancelled
42-61821-62210	CG-4A	390	Unknown		Assembled by Boeing
42-62211-62600	CG-4A	-0-	Not built		Order Cancelled
42-78018	UC-94	(1)	558	NC21942	C-165, impressed
42-78021	UC-77B	(1)	321	NC16402	C-34, impressed
42-78022	UC-94	(1)	562	NC21946	C-165, impressed
42-78023	UC-77D	(1)	381	NC18596	C-37, impressed
42-78024	UC-77D	(1)	366	NC18047	C-37, impressed
42-78025	UC-77B	(1)	309	NC15470	C-34, impressed
42-97412	UC-77D	(1)	347	NC17087	C-37, impressed
42-107400	UC-94	(1)	591	NC32458	C-165, impressed

CESSNA T-50 SERIES MILITARY SERIAL/CONSTRUCTOR'S LIST

MILITARY SERIAL FROM	THRU	MODEL NO.	CESSNA BUILT	CESSNA C/N	REMARKS
41-005	41-037	AT-8	33	1030/1062	AAF
RCAF 7657	7836	CRANE I	180	1100/1279	RCAF
RCAF 7843	7856	CRANE I	14	1286/1299	RCAF
RCAF 7857	7906	CRANE I	50	1350/1399	RCAF
RCAF 7907	8196	CRANE I	290	1400/1689	RCAF
RCAF 8197	8202	CRANE I	6	1280/1285	RCAF
RCAF 8651	8750	CRANE I	100	2201/2300	RCAF
42-2	42-451	AT-17	450	1701/2150	AAF
42-13617	42-13756	CRANE Ia	140	2301/2440	AT-17A Lend-Lease To RCAF As FJ100/239
42-13757	42-13764	AT-17A	8	2441/2448	AAF
42-13765	42-13806	CRANE Ia	42	2449/2490	AT-17A Lend Lease To RCAF As FJ248/289
42-13807	42-13866	AT-17C	60	2491/2550	AAF
42-13867	42-13899	AT-17A	33	2551/2583	AAF
42-13900	42-14030	AT-17D	131	2584/2714	AAF
42-14031	42-14166	UC-78C	136	2715/2850	AAF
42-38276	42-38278	UC-78A	3	1311,1312, 1315	AAF; Impressed T-50
42-38374	42-38375	UC-78A	2	1008, 1005	AAF, Impressed T-50
42-38377	—	UC-78A	1	1018	AAF; Impressed T-50
42-38379	—	UC-78A	1	1001	AAF; Impressed T-50
42-38692	42-39157	AT-17B	466	2901/3366	AAF
42-39158	42-39346	UC-78B	189	3367/3555	AAF
42-43844	—	UC-78A	1	1012	AAF; Impressed T-50
42-58110	42-58439	C-78	330	3601/3930	AAF
42-58440	42-58540	UC-78	101	3931/4031	AAF
42-71465	42-72104	UC-78B	640	4161/4800	AAF
42-72105	42-72164	UC-78C	60	4101/4160	AAF
42-97033	42-97039	UC-78A	7	1314, 1316, 1318/1322	AAF; Impressed T-50
43-7281	43-7377	UC-78	97	4801/4897	AAF
43-7378	43-7384	JRC-1	(7)	4898/4904	USN 55772/55778
43-7385	43-7422	UC-78	38	4905/4942	AAF
43-7423	43-7427	JRC-1	(5)	4943/4947	USN 55779/55783
43-7428	43-7853	UC-78	426*	4948/5373	AAF; *Incl. (55) JRC-1 USN 64442/64496
43-7854	43-8180	UC-78B	327	5374/5700	AAF
43-31763	43-32112	UC-78B	350	5701/6050	AAF
43-32113	43-32762	UC-78B	650	6051/6700	AAF
44-52998	—	C-78A	1	Not Known	AAF; Impressed T-50
44-53001	—	C-78A	1	Not Known	AAF; Impressed T-50

Co-author Bob Pickett spent many years of independent research in the compilation of the tables of production statistics. Many sources were used and the data is as accurate as possible.

C-34 (c/n 314) G-AEAI (John Underwood collection)

C-145 (c/n 457). (John Underwood collection)

C-37, note prop - Harold Martin

C-38 (c/n 412) in 1964. (Peter M. Bowers)

C-37 c/n 385, Finland -Keskinen

C-145 (c/n 462) of Memphis, TN, newspaper.

C-145 unusual markings - Martin

Everybody out! Strength of Airmaster wing.

Proposed T-50 prototype with twin tails!

RCAF Crane I

Group of Crane I's awaiting delivery.

UC-78B, AAF 42-71832, note windows.

JRC-1, BuAer 64456 -H.G. Martin

UC-78B (c/n 6592) Chinese markings in New Delhi, India, Sept. 7, 1945. (Peter M. Bowers photo)

UC-78, XC-BEC (Mexico) in 1954. (Mayborn)

AT-17A (c/n 2377) on floats, 1955. (Bowers)

Frozen brake stopped AT-8, 41-23, Mar. 24, '42.

The C-106 curved to an unplanned stop.

Lower gear next time! AT-8, 41-29, April 25, '42.

Stop quick, lock brakes! AT-8, 41-14, Apr 11, '42.

The Canadians too. Crane I, 7682.

Wind damage to 140, NC76297.

Kamakazi trainer. Direct hit by pilotless AT-17, 42-179 on barn, May 2, 1942.

1948 140 (c/n 14550) N2314V. (Mayborn)

140 (c/n 10871) N76439 in 1962. (Bowers)

140 (c/n 12672) on frozen lake. (Bowers)

140 (c/n 14795) CF-FPJ. (Peter M. Bowers)

"Discover Flying" paint scheme on 1968 150H.

1973 FRA150L Aerobat (130 hp) made in France.

Gulp! 1971 150L for shipment in C-124.

1971 A150L Aerobat (c/n A1500227) at work.

1917 Comet and Clyde Cessna at Wichita "factory."

Multi-named Design No. 2 as c/n 1627.

Beautiful airplanes and girls go together.

Cessna's trademark on C-37 prototype (c/n 330).

140 c/n 8173, NC89161 -H.Martin

Early 140 with floats.

1949 140A (c/n 15242) with Continental C-90.

End of the line. Another T-50 wastes away.